# PRAY IN THE SPIRIT

# PRAY IN THE SPIRIT

*The Work of the Holy Spirit
in the Ministry of Prayer*

ARTHUR WALLIS

**CHRISTIAN LITERATURE CRUSADE**
Fort Washington, Pennsylvania 19034

CHRISTIAN LITERATURE CRUSADE

U.S.A.
Box 1449, Fort Washington, PA 19034

GREAT BRITAIN
51 The Dean, Alresford, Hants., SO24 9BJ

AUSTRALIA
P.O. Box 91, Pennant Hills, N.S.W. 2120

NEW ZEALAND
P.O. Box 1203, Palmerston North

© Arthur Wallis 1970

First American Edition 1977
under special arrangements with
Kingsway Publications Ltd.
Eastbourne, Sussex, England

This printing 1993 (New Jacket)

*Cover photo: J. Tinier*

*ISBN 0-87508-561-X*

All Rights Reserved. No part of this publication may be
translated, reproduced, or transmitted in any form or
by any means, electronic or mechanical, including
photocopy, recording, or any information storage and
retrieval system, without permission in writing from the
publisher.

PRINTED IN COLOMBIA

# CONTENTS

To a true and devoted helpmeet—who has so often behind the scenes held up my drooping hands—with deep gratitude.

Scripture quotations are from the
Revised Standard Version

# PREFACE

A MAN is no bigger than his prayer life, or as Murray M'Cheyne is reputed to have said, 'What a man is on his knees before God, that he is—and nothing more.' In that coming day when the hearts of men are revealed, a day which is now nearer than when we first believed, there will be some 'big men' who will appear very small, and some we had thought small will appear as spiritual giants. How different are spiritual values when God takes them from the balances of human judgment and weighs them on the balances of the sanctuary.

The swift and powerful movement of the Spirit recorded in the Acts was not only initiated by prayer, but fed and sustained by prayer. In a day when God has begun to pour out His Spirit upon His people, even as He promised, we should expect to see among them a new 'spirit of grace and supplication'. However powerful the initial coming upon us of the Spirit may be, if this does not find expression in a life of prayer the blessing will soon become a fading glory. A movement of God will last as long as the Spirit of prayer that inspired it.

The result of the Holy Spirit coming upon a believer should be that he is introduced to *life in the Spirit*. In this new dimension every spiritual activity is energized and controlled by the Spirit of God. Living in the Spirit includes praying in the Spirit. Any claim to a baptism or filling with the Spirit which leaves our prayer life unaffected must be at best a superficial work, for the Holy Spirit of promise is an indwelling intercessor. He comes to each heart open to Him with a deep longing to find there another channel through which to effect this powerful ministry.

This is not intended to be a general book on prayer. It concentrates on the ministry of the Holy Spirit in relation to prayer. It investigates the deeper meaning of that apostolic injunction, 'Pray in the Spirit.' It analyses our many weaknesses in prayer and the spiritual and practical difficulties we encounter, and shows how the Holy Spirit helps us in our weakness and makes up for all our deficiency. It encourages us to yield ourselves to Him and allow Him to pray through us. We need have no fear that this will make us unbalanced or extreme. The more fully we submit to the Holy Spirit the more Christ-centred we become, and the more truly God is glorified in us.

What tremendous possibilities there are when we have plunged into that river of the Spirit which is full of water. Here are 'waters to swim in'. Prayer in the Spirit suggests new avenues waiting to be explored, new resources to be tapped, new power to be released. And when we have begun to enter into all that is opened up in these pages, we shall realize, reader and author alike, how much there is of 'the deep things of God' still waiting to be discovered.

*There the Lord in majesty will be for us a place of broad rivers and streams, where no galley with oars can go,* [no room here for human energy,] *nor stately ship can pass.* [no place for fleshly show or ostentation] (Isa. 33 : 21).

May God use this book to help us to launch out.

ARTHUR WALLIS

## I

# BUT HOW?

SHE was young, she was of lowly birth and, what made it even more perplexing, she was unmarried. Could she be hearing aright? Chosen by heaven to be the mother of the long-awaited Messiah? Doubt, fear, perplexity struggled within her. Turning to the angel Mary asked a simple, practical question, 'How can this be?' Just as simple was Gabriel's answer, 'The Holy Spirit will come upon you.' 'How?' is a question that the believer is for ever asking, even if only deep in the heart. To our every 'How?' heaven gives the same answer as Gabriel gave to Mary—'The Holy Spirit.'

Is it a question of how we may know the will of God in our lives? 'All who are led by the Spirit of God are sons of God.' Are we concerned to know the secret of victory over sin? 'The law of the Spirit of life in Christ Jesus has set me free from the law of sin and death.' Have we difficulty in understanding the Scriptures? 'The Holy Spirit . . . will teach you all things.' 'The Spirit of truth . . . will guide you into all the truth.' Is it the problem of how to witness effectively for the Lord? 'You shall receive power when the Holy Spirit has come upon you; and you shall be My witnesses.'

Perhaps the fact that we have picked up a book

on the subject of prayer is an indication that we are wanting to know *how to pray* aright, how to prevail in prayer. 'The Spirit helps us in our weakness,' replies the apostle. 'The Spirit Himself intercedes for us.' The gracious ministry of the Holy Spirit is God's complete answer to all our weakness, ignorance and inability in the realm of prayer.

In the Upper Room discourse (John 14–16) our Lord gave His followers their fullest unfolding of the promised Holy Spirit. In five great declarations He revealed what the Holy Spirit was to be to them and to do for them. It is significant that in the same passage we find some five or six great prayer promises. It was through the Holy Spirit that they would find the prayer promises fulfilled. Further, the distinctive title our Lord gave to the Holy Spirit was 'The Comforter' or 'The Advocate', a title that would have suggested to the disciples a ministry of intercession. Our Lord wanted them to know that the Holy Spirit was an intercessor, and that He would accomplish this ministry in them.

The early church was without doubt a praying church, and what tremendous things they accomplished through prayer alone: prison doors were opened, fanatical opponents were struck down and converted to Christ, signs and wonders were done. But the open secret was that the early church knew the presence and power of the Holy Spirit, not theoretically but experientially. Those first believers were mighty in prayer because they were mighty in the Spirit.

We have only to scan the pages of The Acts to discover that the early church met and overcame every great crisis in their early history with the weapon of 'all prayer'. Read, in Acts 4, that account of the first recorded prayer meeting of the young Jerusalem Church for an example of anointed praying. What boldness! What power! What authority! Little wonder the place where they were assembled was shaken and they were all filled anew with the Holy Spirit. So the enduement of the Spirit was both the cause and the consequence of their effectual praying. They prayed because they were filled, and they were filled because they prayed. A victorious circle!

In a day when an increasing number of God's children are recognizing the necessity of a vital encounter with the Holy Spirit, let us always keep before us this prayer aspect of the Spirit-filled life. In Ezekiel's vision (chapter 47) the waters that flowed out of the sanctuary were firstly 'ankle-deep', which suggests walking in the Spirit; and then 'knee-deep', which suggests praying in the Spirit. There is a serious deficiency in the outworking of the Spirit-filled life if it does not issue in a revitalizing experience in the realm of prayer.

When the Lord met with me in this way some years ago, He touched many realms of my spiritual life, but none more deeply and permanently than my prayer life, though I realize there is still a long way to go. If someone should ask, 'How do you know what spirit came upon you?' I would reply, 'By the fruit produced. I soon discovered that the Spirit that had come upon me was an interceding Spirit.'

Praying in the Spirit summarizes in a phrase the New Testament norm for the believer's prayer life. This in turn assumes a definite reception of the Spirit in fullness and power. Our blessed Lord knew this experience, and so did those apostles and believers of the early churches. Everywhere the New Testament writers take it for granted (as they do baptism in water) that their readers have known this rich experience of the Holy Spirit coming upon them (Titus 3 : 5, 6). Today, alas, it cannot be so readily assumed. But without such an experience what follows in this book will be largely theoretical and unreal.

I would invite the reader who is unconvinced of the necessity of such a definite experience, but who is open to the testimony of God's word, to carry out a simple investigation. With the help of a concordance examine all the references in the New Testament to being filled with the Spirit, and see whether there is not overwhelming evidence that this is a distinct and definite encounter with the Holy Spirit, and that those who experienced it in New Testament times knew when and how the Holy Spirit had come. Paul could never have asked the Galatians, 'Did you receive the Spirit by works of the law, or by hearing with faith?' if their experience of receiving the Spirit had not been at least as clearly defined as their experience of receiving Christ.

Let others who, though convinced of the scripturalness and importance of it, are still strangers to the experience, come with purity of heart, cleanness of hands, and simplicity of faith to the risen Lord. He is still calling out, 'If any man thirst let him come to Me and drink.' So come and drink, for the promise is to you.

## 2

## THE TWO ADVOCATES

THERE is only one place in the Bible where we are given any insight into the work of the Holy Spirit as intercessor, and that is Romans 8 : 26, 27 :

> Likewise the Spirit helps us in our weakness; for we do not know how to pray as we ought, but the Spirit Himself intercedes for us with sighs too deep for words. And He who searches the hearts of men knows what is the mind of the Spirit, because the Spirit intercedes for the saints according to the will of God.

A few verses farther on we are introduced to Another who also intercedes for us (verse 34) :

> Christ Jesus, who died, yes, who was raised from the dead, who is at the right hand of God, who indeed intercedes for us.

So the Holy Spirit intercedes for us, and Christ Jesus intercedes for us. It is important to see that these two intercessions, though related, are quite distinct. There is no duplication in the various activities of the persons of the Godhead. It is certain that we shall never understand how the Holy Spirit intercedes for us unless we distinguish His ministry as intercessor from that of our great High Priest.

When Jesus introduced to His disciples the distinct promise of the Holy Spirit, He said: 'I will pray the Father, and He will give you another Counsellor, to be with you for ever' (John 14 : 16). As for this word 'counsellor', otherwise rendered 'comforter' or 'advocate', there is probably no word in English that fully conveys the original and covers the same breadth of meaning, hence the tendency to anglicize the Greek word by rendering it as 'Paraclete'. Its primitive meaning is 'one called to the side of' another to help him.[1] 'It was used in a court of justice to denote a legal assistant, counsel for the defence, an advocate.'[2] Certainly this connection with the law courts is not now conveyed by 'comforter' (A.V. and R.V.) though that lovely word does cover another aspect of the Holy Spirit's ministry.

When Jesus told the disciples that He would ask the Father to send them 'another Paraclete', He used a word signifying 'another of the same kind.'[3] It was as though He was saying, 'I alone have been your Paraclete up to the present, but the Father will send you another like Me, even the Holy Spirit, whose abiding presence you shall have to the end of the age.' Though Christ was no longer to be with them personally, He would not cease to be their Paraclete, their heavenly barrister, to represent them in the court of heaven. It is the same John who recorded these words who tells us in his first epistle, 'If any one does sin, we have a Paraclete [same word] with the Father, Jesus

Christ the righteous' (2 : 1). So the disciples were not really losing their Paraclete, except in bodily presence; they were gaining another like Him. <u>We now have two heavenly Advocates, both of whom are said to intercede for us.</u>

Suppose a man decides to settle some dispute by litigation. His case may be good, but he knows nothing of court procedure, or how to carry his case by debate and argument. He is incapable of presenting the facts so as to convince the judge, so he calls to his aid a barrister who accepts the man as his client, and conducts the case on his behalf. So do these two divine Advocates, though in different ways.

Notice that there is a difference in the location of these two intercessors. Christ intercedes 'at the right hand of God' (Rom. 8 : 34). He is our 'advocate with the Father' (1 John 2 : 1). The Holy Spirit on the other hand intercedes in the hearts of men (Rom. 8 : 27). Christ's intercession is apart from us, the Holy Spirit's is within us. We cannot help, nor can we hinder the intercession of Christ Jesus, our great High Priest. Whether we follow hard after Him or follow afar off; whether we are hot or cold, spiritual or carnal, His intercession continues unceasingly. 'I am praying . . . for those whom Thou hast given Me' (John 17 : 9). Nothing we do can touch that intercession, for it proceeds on the ground of what He has done for us. His death and resurrection, not what we have done or are doing for Him. It is therefore not affected by our ups and downs. What an encouragement to know that He has inscribed our names on His 'prayer list' for all time.

When we turn to the intercession of the Spirit the position is very different. It is a solemn fact that we may facilitate or frustrate the Spirit's intercession in us, by our co-operation or the lack of it. Though Christ does not require us for His intercession, the Holy Spirit most assuredly does for His. Here we can no longer be spectators, we must be participators. Christ prays for us in the sense that He makes us the *object* of His praying. The Holy Spirit prays for us in the sense that He makes us the *vehicle* of His praying. He prays on our behalf by enabling us to pray, helping us in our weakness, who do not know how to pray as we ought.

The life truly possessed by the Holy Spirit is the indispensable channel of the Spirit's intercession. There appears to be no suggestion in Scripture that the Holy Spirit ever intercedes except through the believer. This is emphasized in Romans 8 : 15, 16 in the R.S.V. by an interesting variation in punctuation: 'When we cry "Abba! Father!" it is the Spirit Himself bearing witness with our spirit that we are children of God.' Notice what Paul is saying, 'When we cry . . . it is the Spirit.' We do the crying, but the Holy Spirit does the inspiring of the cry. Compare this with the day of Pentecost when 'they began to speak . . . as the Spirit gave them utterance' (Acts 2 : 4). Notice that Romans 8 : 16 does *not* say that the Spirit bears witness *to* our spirit, but *with* our spirit. The divine Spirit and the human spirit become joint witnesses by the cry that comes from within us.

All this is borne out by other aspects of the Spirit's ministry. He is a witnessing Spirit, but this witnessing He effects through the believer (John 15:26, 27; Acts 5:32). He is a convicting Spirit, but this is 'when He comes' 'unto you' (John 16:7, 8). He is a wooing Spirit, but not apart from the Bride (Rev. 22:17).

The Holy Spirit needs us to accomplish His intercessory ministry, and we certainly need Him to accomplish ours. What a privilege to be invited to join in this heavenly partnership. He wants to be free to think through our minds, feel through our hearts, speak through our lips, and even weep through our eyes and groan through our spirits. When a believer is thus at the disposal of the Holy Spirit, praying in the Spirit will be a reality.

[1] *Parakletos* from *para*, beside, and *kaleo*, to call.
[2] Vine's Expository Dictionary of N.T. Words.
[3] Greek *allos*.

# 3

## IN THE SPIRIT

To understand rightly the expression 'Pray in the Spirit' we must first understand what Scripture means by 'in the Spirit', for it is used not only in connection with prayer. It is necessary to define our terms carefully as there has been a tendency in some quarters to assume too readily that *praying in the Spirit* and *praying with the spirit* are identical terms. This latter expression, found only in 1 Corinthians 14:15, denotes praying in tongues, as the context clearly shows. Failing to distinguish the two terms, some have concluded that praying in the Spirit is limited to praying in tongues. In fact praying in tongues is but one of three distinct kinds of praying in the Spirit mentioned in Scripture.

*int.*

Examination of the above reference in Corinthians with the two references to praying 'in the Spirit' or 'in the Holy Spirit' (Eph. 6:18 and Jude 20) indicate that they are not synonymous. There is a difference in the Greek which our translators have been careful to convey by not only using different prepositions, 'with' and 'in', but by using a capital 'S' for 'in the Spirit' and a small 's' for 'with the spirit', and that is true of all the main versions.

Take the expression, 'Pray with the spirit.' If we

follow Paul's argument we shall see that 'spirit' here refers to the human spirit. He says:

> If I pray in a tongue, *my* spirit prays but my mind is unfruitful. What am I to do? I will pray with the [my] spirit and I will pray with the [my] mind also.

It is in the realm of the human spirit that the spiritual gift operates. In fact so closely is the human spirit identified with the spiritual gift in the minds of the New Testament writers that they seem to use the one where we would have expected the other. For example, Paul commends the Corinthians that they were 'eager for manifestations of the Spirit' (1 Cor. 14:12. 'spiritual gifts' A.V., R.V.), but the original says that they were 'eager for spirits'. Similarly, John says 'Test the spirits to see whether they are of God ... every spirit which confesses that Jesus Christ has come in the flesh is of God' (1 John 4:1, 2). What could be meant by 'every spirit which ... is of God'? It surely refers to the human spirit manifesting a spiritual gift, such as prophecy. Again, 'the seven spirits who are before His throne' (Rev. 1:14) must mean seven manifestations of the one divine Spirit, as in Isaiah 11:12.

It is clear, then, that in 1 Corinthians 14 praying with the spirit is equivalent to praying with the spiritual gift. This involves the human spirit as distinct from the human mind. The emphasis here is not on the Holy Spirit, as with the expression 'in the Spirit', though of course His presence and activity are implied, for we cannot pray rightly with the spirit, or even with the mind for that matter, apart from the Holy Spirit. But it is important to see where the emphasis lies.

Let us take this comparison further. Paul says, 'I will pray with the spirit and I will pray with the mind also.' The repetition, 'I will pray ... and I will pray ...' proves that Paul envisages two kinds of praying, not as some have supposed, the human spirit and the human mind praying together. He means that he will pray with his new tongue (Mk. 16:17) and he will pray with his native tongue. But in Ephesians 6:18 he exhorts us 'Pray *at all times* in the Spirit.' So praying is only sometimes 'with the spirit' (i.e. in tongues) but 'at all times in the Spirit'.

Paul contrasts 'in the Spirit' with 'in the flesh' (Rom. 8:9). So the alternative to 'praying in the Spirit' is praying in the flesh. No wonder he says, 'Pray *at all times* in the Spirit.' But in 1 Corinthians 14 the contrast is between praying 'with the spirit' and praying 'with the mind', both of which may be 'in the Spirit' and pleasing to God. 'In the Spirit' is therefore a much broader concept than 'with the spirit.' To identify the one with the other is to imply that all the great intercessors of the Old Testament and even our blessed Lord Himself did not pray in the Spirit because, to our knowledge, they did not pray in tongues.

Now prayer is not the only activity 'in the Spirit' required of us. The New Testament speaks of living in the Spirit, walking in the Spirit, worshipping in the Spirit, joying in the Spirit, etc. All that is meant is that each activity is performed by the power and enabling of the Holy Spirit. This is in exact agreement with what we have already learned is meant by praying in the Spirit. Expressed in the most practical terms it means that the Holy Spirit inspires, guides, energizes and sustains the praying.

The contexts of the only two references to praying in the Spirit in the New Testament are instructive. The first reference concludes that great passage in Ephesians 6 on the armour of God in the believer's warfare. The other, in Jude, follows the exhortation to build ourselves up on our most holy faith. So it is in the context of battling and building that we are exhorted to 'pray in the Spirit'. These two figures in fact sum up what the Christian life is all about. We are reminded of Nehemiah and his compatriots engaged in their God-given task of restoring Jerusalem, sword in one hand and trowel in the other. Our Lord emphasized these two aspects when He spoke of the necessity of first counting the cost before committing ourselves to the path of discipleship. He used the twin parable of the man intending to build a tower and the king going out to battle against another king (Luke 14:28–32). So discipleship too is a matter of building and battling. If we are to build to a successful conclusion and to wage a victorious warfare against our implacable foe we must learn to pray in the Spirit.

# 4

## HELPING OUR WEAKNESS

I don't seem to have any real desire for prayer.
I do it more out of a sense of duty than anything
else.
When I pray I feel as though God is a million
miles away. I don't seem to have any real assurance that He hears me, and that I am truly talking to Him.
I pray but nothing ever seems to happen. I get so
discouraged and feel, What's the use?
I suffer from wandering thoughts in prayer and
cannot seem to concentrate.

SUCH remarks are commonly expressed by believers both young and old, and provide a living
commentary on what the apostle says concerning
'our weakness' in prayer, and the fact that 'we do
not know how to pray as we ought' (Rom. 8:26).
Most of us are very ready to acknowledge the truth
of this. We strive to pray more often, more fer-
vently, more believingly. Challenging ministry on
the subject stimulates us to fresh resolve. The bio-
graphy of a man of prayer stirs us up. Some pressing need in our lives drives us to our knees, and for
a while we pray with greater feeling and fervour,
only to slide back sooner or later to the drudgery
and even monotony of our old prayer life.

It may come as a word of hope to some child of God, discouraged by the hardness of the way, that the great apostle was not merely referring to weaker Christians, to those young in the faith, or to the spiritually immature when he said, 'We do not know how to pray.' He used the word 'we' and so included himself. He is making a statement which must in the very nature of the case, be universally true of every believer. We are inherently, inevitably and incorrigibly weak when it comes to prayer, and we never can be otherwise.

Paul had come to see this in his own experience, not by reasoning but by revelation. But many Christians who are ever bemoaning their inadequate prayer life have never had this revelation. That is why they strive and struggle to demonstrate to themselves and to God that they are not really so weak after all. Setting themselves to disprove divine facts, the battle is lost before it has begun. The way through is not to be found along these lines.

Of course Paul's discovery of his own weakness was not only related to prayer but to the whole business of living a life that was pleasing to God. Some account of how he arrived there is given in the very context of the verse we are now considering, the latter part of Romans 7 and the beginning of chapter 8. Elsewhere he speaks of other experiences that brought home the same great principle, as when he prayed unsuccessfully for the removal of his 'thorn in the flesh', and God said, 'My power is made perfect in weakness' (2 Cor. 12 : 9). When the Holy Spirit brings home to us this truth of our insufficiency, we shall bow and accept it, and prove with Paul that it is not *out of* weakness (that is, the thorn removed), but *in* weakness that God's power is made perfect. Even so in prayer, 'the Spirit helps us *in* our weakness'.

Some know 'the rest of utter weakness' and others only know the striving of utter weakness. The one is a thing of faith, the other a thing of works; the one a thing of the Spirit, the other a thing of the flesh. It is, after all, only the pride of our own hearts that causes us to rebel against this innate weakness, to strive to escape from its clutches and attain a place of strength, of independence, of self-sufficiency. It seems to cut right across our efforts to achieve self-significance. How wonderful it is when we discover, often through the discipline of repeated failure, that this weakness with which we seem to be permanently saddled is not 'the end', but a new and wonderful beginning—the gateway to heaven's resources. 'The Spirit helps us in our weakness.' The weakness is perpetual only that we might be perpetually dependent on the Holy Spirit.

The word 'help' used here is the translation of one of those fascinating compound verbs so difficult to convey adequately in the English. It is found in only one other passage, Luke 10:40, where Martha complains to the Lord about her sister leaving her to do all the work: 'Tell her then to *help* me.' Primarily the word means 'to take hold of', but it has a double prefix, meaning 'together with.' and 'instead of'. This may at first seem to be a contradiction in terms, to say that the Spirit 'takes hold of [our weakness], together with, instead of'. We have in fact a marvellous truth, not merely that the Spirit intervenes in our weakness, but that He does so 'together with' us—for He requires our willing co-operation—and 'instead of' us, for He does for us what we could never do for ourselves.

In the following chapters we shall be examining some of the weaknesses we experience in prayer, and seeing how the Holy Spirit helps us in each one, as we trust Him and obey Him.

## THAT APATHETIC SPIRIT

AN obvious reason why many of us do not pray when we should and as we should is lack of desire. A spiritual lethargy and inertia seem to settle upon us with paralysing effect. The excuse may be that we are too busy to pray; the fact is, as we well know, we always find time for what we want to do, and are only too busy for what we don't want to do and don't have to do. Apathy is perhaps the major reason why the prayer life of so many professed believers is minimal—just enough to maintain, at least in their own eyes, their Christian respectability (horrible phrase!) and clear themselves of the charge of backsliding. Lack of desire means that prayer is perfunctory and legalistic, a duty instead of a delight.

Now this state of heart may be caused by sin. If we have a controversy with our Lord, if we are rebelling against the Holy Spirit, if we have not performed our vows, or if we have allowed envy, bitterness or anger to mar our feelings towards our fellows—such things as these are enough to bring a pall of death over our times of fellowship with God. The remedy is in our own hands: 'If we confess our sins, He is faithful and just, and will forgive our sins and cleanse us from all unrighteousness.' The proof that the sin was the cause of our barren prayer life is that when it is confessed we find ourselves out of the shadows, and once again in the sunlight of God's presence.

But what of those who tell us that they have confessed and dealt with all that God has shown them, and still there is no real desire? This is a chronic spiritual state with many, and it must be recognized as part of our weakness in the realm of prayer. But let us not be discouraged. God knows all about this kind of weakness in the heart of one who has a real longing for a vital prayer experience. The Spirit has been given to help us in our weakness.

It is obvious that we cannot be possessed by a spirit of fervent intercession, and at the same time by a spirit of lethargy in prayer. The Spirit that God has given us is an interceding Spirit. It is He who inspired every prayer that ever reached God's throne and brought down heaven's blessing. He is the great Advocate who produces within us a spirit of intercession, if we will but trust Him to do so. 'Because you are sons, God has sent the Spirit of His Son into our hearts, crying "Abba! Father!"' (Gal. 4:6).

Let us confess to the sin of indifference and neglect in relation to this ministry of the Holy Spirit. Let us confess to the sin of unbelief in that we have so often acted as though there were no Holy Spirit. If He has not filled and possessed us, we must begin right here, and ask Him to do so now. If He has, let us believe that as we yield ourselves afresh to Him He takes full possession as an interceding Spirit, to do His work in us and through us. Remember the lesson of Romans 8:26. 'The Spirit helps *with us* and *instead of us*.'

The verse from Galatians, quoted above, tells us that the Spirit that God sent forth into our hearts, crying "Abba! Father!" is *the Spirit of His Son*. This is the Spirit that came upon our Lord at the Jordan in the form of a dove. This is the Spirit that rested upon Him as He continued all night in prayer on the lonely mountain side. This is the same Spirit that moved Him to rise a great while before it was day and go out into a solitary place to pray. This was no ritual, no legal duty that He was performing. There was a great hunger in the heart of the Son of Man for fellowship with His God and Father. The Spirit of His Son in you will create a like hunger, if you will but give Him liberty to do so.

If before you felt as though a team of horses could scarcely drag you to the place of prayer, now you will feel as though a team of horses could scarce drag you away. What a difference it is when we come to the place of prayer as a lover to the meeting place, or when, like Hannah, we pray with the burden of prayer upon us, and pour out our soul before the Lord.

# GETTING THROUGH TO GOD

PERHAPS it is our experience that when we pray God seems very far away. We feel that our praying is like speaking into the air or talking down a dead telephone line. In that case our weakness focuses on this problem of 'getting through to God', or, to use the biblical word, the problem of 'access'. The Bible has a lot to say about this, for the truths about access to God and fellowship with God lie at the heart of our salvation. There are two aspects to this matter that we must consider. The first is generally known and understood by believers, but it needs to be restated as it provides the basis of the second aspect which is often completely overlooked. Let us call the first aspect—

## THE RIGHT OF ACCESS

God made man for His own pleasure, that He might enjoy fellowship with His creatures. But sin came, and with it separation from God. An iron curtain, more terrible than that which separates East from West, fell between the holy God and His sinning creatures. The message of the Bible reveals how God dealt with that dread curtain through Jesus Christ to bring man back to His original purpose. 'For there is one God, and there is one mediator between God and men, the man Christ Jesus' (1 Tim. 2:5).

What hope could there be of man ever approaching that throne of God's holiness without the presence and work of the mediator Christ Jesus? He said Himself, 'No one comes to the Father, but by Me' (John 14:6). What does this mean? Simply that Christ's death, resurrection and ascension have torn the curtain apart and opened a way for man into the otherwise inaccessible presence of God. Peter the apostle puts it this way:

> For Christ also died for sins once for all, the righteous for the unrighteous, that He might bring us to God (1 Pet. 3:18).

This picture of a curtain of separation is in fact the very one that the Bible uses. In Old Testament times there was a curtain (or veil) that separated the Holy Place where the priests ministered from the inner sanctuary or Holy of Holies where dwelt the concentrated glory of God's presence in both the tabernacle and the temple. This was to show that the way was not yet open for man to have direct personal access to God (Heb. 9:8). No man could pass beyond that curtain on pain of death, the only exception being the High Priest; he was permitted to do so once a year, but not without the blood of sacrifice.

The gospel record tells us that when Jesus died a strange portent took place within the temple. The curtain separating the Holy Place from the

Holy of Holies was torn in two, and the record is careful to add, 'from top to bottom', to emphasize that it was no act of man that performed this, but an act of God (Mat. 27:51). The way into the presence of God had been opened at last. How beautifully this is expressed in the epistle to the Hebrews (10:19–22):

> Therefore, brethren, since we have confidence to enter the sanctuary by the blood of Jesus, by the new and living way which He opened for us through the curtain, that is, through His flesh ... let us draw near ...

The curtain (or veil) represented the invisible barrier separating God and man on account of sin. When Jesus died on the cross He took that sin barrier on Himself, bearing our sins in His own body (1 Pet. 2:24), and so fully was He identified with our sin that God was said to have 'made Him to be sin who knew no sin' (2 Cor. 5:21). Thus the crucifying of that sinless body was looked upon as a tearing of the curtain of separation, and the opening of a way into the presence of God for us.

This work of Christ as mediator is a truth that became obscured in the medieval era of the church, but was brought fully into the light by the Reformation, and is dear to the heart of all true believers. We need no human priest or intermediary, for we have one great High Priest in the presence of God for us. Through Him every believer has the right of direct access to God.

It is good to be reminded that we can never approach God, whether in prayer or praise, supplication or intercession, except through Christ.

If then we have this *right of access* as believers, how can there be any problem in getting through to God in prayer? Why is it that we find those who, knowing and believing that they have this right to enter into God's presence through Christ, find themselves faced with a practical problem in the outworking of it? The right to draw near with boldness does not seem to ensure a living audience with the King. Despite all that people say, despite all that they themselves believe, their prayer life remains dull and lifeless, and the God whom they address is a God afar off.

Of course the simple explanation may be a matter that we have touched on already. Even though we have the right of access we are still required to come with clean hands and a pure heart into God's presence. Only by the confession of known sin, and the thorough renunciation of it does the death of Christ and the power of His blood avail for us as we draw near to God. Otherwise, by countenancing sin in our hearts, we stop God's ears (Isa. 59:2; Psa. 66:18). Any form of disobedience may easily produce an impenetrable barrier to our prayers, and keep us out of touch with God. Where we are conscious of 'something between' but do not know what it is, the Holy Spirit is ready and waiting to reveal it, if we will only seek the Lord. Where we do know, the remedy is simple; we must tread the humbling pathway of confession, renunciation and maybe restitution, and so be restored to God's fellowship.

But what of those who have genuinely examined themselves before God without being convicted of any specific sin that could account for their inability to get through to God? The solution is found, I believe, in the second aspect of this truth. This we will call:

## THE POWER OF ACCESS

We may say that *the right of access* is the result of the work of Christ, and *the power of access* is the result of the work of the Holy Spirit. Both are included by Paul when he says:

For through Him [Christ] we both [Jew and Gentile] have *access in one Spirit* to the Father (Eph. 2 : 18).

This phrase, 'access in one Spirit', teaches us that the Holy Spirit has a vital part to play in our getting through to God. What Christ has accomplished *for us* by providing us with the right of access, the Spirit must now work *in us* by providing us with the power of access. Paul is teaching us here that our access to God through Christ is in the power of, or through the working of, one Spirit, even the Spirit of God. In other words, the same Spirit that proceeds from God is available to conduct us to God. In fact all our fellowship with God is dependent upon the gracious activity of this one Spirit. We should be reminded of this every time we hear the benediction pronounced, concluding with the words, 'the fellowship of the Holy Spirit be with you all' (2 Cor. 13:14). It is a fellowship with the Father and with His Son Jesus Christ effected and maintained by the Holy Spirit.

If a man is summoned to the king's palace to receive some decoration, the royal summons is his right to enter the king's presence. It takes him past the sentries and officers of the guard who would otherwise debar him from the palace. But having gained entry he would be at a loss to find his way into the sovereign's presence if left to himself in that labyrinth of corridors. He needs a palace attendant to conduct him personally to the audience chamber. The work of Christ provides us with the royal summons and constitutes our right of entry, but the indwelling Spirit is also needed to conduct us into God's presence. It is His work to make access to God a reality; to bring to us the deep conviction that we are not talking into the air when we pray, but communing face to face with a loving heavenly Father.

The Holy Spirit thus provides the answer to our weakness in this matter of getting through to God, for He makes our praying a conscious experience of fellowship with God. What a wonderful thing is 'the fellowship of the Holy Spirit'. Let us draw near to God and pray with the full assurance of faith that the Holy Spirit will indeed help us in our weakness. 'The Lord God is a sun' (Psa. 84:11), and when we commune with Him in the Spirit we shall be conscious of a spiritual warmth pervading our beings, and when we go our way, like Moses descending the mount, we shall be unconsciously reflecting something of the glory.

## 7

# KNOWING GOD'S WILL

ANOTHER obvious and serious weakness from which we all suffer in the realm of prayer is that in so many situations we have to admit that we do not know the will of God. The Authorized (or King James') Version puts it this way: 'We know not what we should pray for' (Rom. 8:26). Later versions: 'We do not know how to pray.' We may apply this to the subject matter of our praying. When we get beyond the well-worn paths, having prayed for our families and friends, our churches and fellow-Christians, servants of God at home and overseas, there are still endless needs and possibilities for intercession. If we try to cover every need and respond to every call our prayer life becomes a river without a river bed, that flows here, there, and everywhere, until its energy is swallowed up in a marsh. Here is a basic rule: if intercession is to be effective it must be selective. But here lies our problem, 'We know not what we should pray for . . .'

Even on those occasions when we do know what we should pray for, there is a real problem as to how we should pray for it. For example, an elderly believer, who has been in failing health for some time, is taken seriously ill and is not expected to live. How should we pray for him? We have to face the possibility that his time on earth is done. In that case, for us to pray with all the faith and zeal we can muster for his restoration to health would be to pray contrary to the mind of God, and our hope would certainly be disappointed. This kind of thing often happens.

Let us take another case. There is the problem of the church member who it seems is bent on making trouble and causing division. Should we pray for him to be restored or removed? During her time at missionary training college my wife, together with one or two other students, used to help in a mission situated in a rather notorious district of London. In the childrens' meetings there was a disruptive element, and she wrote me of her quandary as to how to pray for these little hooligans—'for grace to keep them in, or for strength to chuck them out'! How true it is of so many situations, 'We do not know how to pray.'

Of course many find an easy way of escape from this kind of dilemma. They pray for whatever they think best, and then qualify it with—'if it be Thy will'. This is particularly the case when it comes to prayer for the sick, and it is generally looked upon as signifying commendable submission to the unknown will of God, or perhaps by others as the best that is possible under the circumstances. Among the many examples of Bible prayers, this kind is conspicuous by its absence. How can a hit-or-miss prayer of this sort be in faith? And if not in faith how can it be pleasing to God? The New Testament does not encourage us to wander on in our ignorance, it emphasizes the need of being 'filled with the knowledge of His will' (Col. 1:9); it commands us to 'understand what the will of the Lord is' (Eph. 5:17); it exhorts us to 'prove what is the will of God' (Rom. 12:2).

The apostle John writes:

And this is the confidence which we have in Him, that if we ask anything according to His will He hears us. And if we know that He hears us in whatever we ask, we know that we have obtained the requests made of Him (1 John 5:14, 15).

Now if we are always falling back on to the safety of these 'if-it-be-Thy-will prayers' we are debasing this most well-known prayer promise of the apostle John, and making it a prayer 'let-out', a useful carpet under which we can sweep all our unanswered prayers. We imply that what he is really saying is this: 'And this is the lack of confidence which we have in Him, that unless we happen to ask according to His will, He will *not* hear us, and we shall not have our petition.' So the promise that was intended to confirm our faith serves only to cover our unbelief and to confirm us in our state of weakness, in seeking to prevail with God.

How then are we to reconcile these two facts —we are ignorant of the will of God, and yet, in order to receive, are required to pray according to it? Here is a weakness serious enough to render all our praying ineffectual. But the apostle points us to this wonderful fact that Someone has been sent to help us who has a perfect knowledge of the will of God. 'The Spirit helps us in our weakness . . . the Spirit Himself intercedes for us . . . the Spirit intercedes for the saints according to the will of God.'

We have already seen that this same Spirit creates desire within us for such fellowship with God; that He not only proceeds from God but is available to conduct us to God. Now we see that He is able to make up for all our deficiencies in understanding God's will. There must of necessity be perfect harmony between the mind of God and the mind of the Spirit. How wonderful that He has sent forth His Spirit into our hearts, to help our weakness, to supply our lack, to do for us what we cannot do for ourselves. How vital that we depend on Him to do this work.

All this is but another aspect of that promise of our Lord concerning the Holy Spirit, 'He shall teach you all things'—all things that you need to know to fulfil your ministry. When the disciples said to Jesus, 'Lord teach us to pray,' He gave them their first lesson by teaching them the Lord's prayer. When we now ask Him to teach us to pray He points us to the Holy Spirit, and says, 'He will teach you.'

But we may well ask, 'How *does* the Holy Spirit teach us to pray according to God's will?' Not by imparting facts and then leaving us to get on with the job, but by interceding for us, with us and in us. Once I wanted a small adjustment done on the engine of my car. I phoned my friend who not only knows all about cars but also of my ignorance about them! He could have given me instructions over the phone which might, or might not, have proved successful. Instead he graciously came and did the job for me. 'The Spirit Himself intercedes for us ... the Spirit intercedes for the saints according to the will of God.'

This interceding Spirit dwelling within us is also 'the Spirit of wisdom and understanding, the Spirit of counsel and might, the Spirit of knowledge and of the fear of the Lord' (Isa. 11:2). As we pray He is waiting to be to us our fountain of wisdom, understanding, counsel, might, knowledge and fear of the Lord. Later we shall discuss the practical ways in which He guides and inspires us to pray according to God's will, and how in practice we are to co-operate with Him.

## 8

## WHEN FAITH WOULD FAIL

LACK of faith is one of the most obvious and prevalent weaknesses in the realms of prayer. Of course this is closely related to what has just been said about knowing the will of God, for one Scripture assures us that we must pray according to God's will, if we are to receive, another that we must pray in faith. But even in the well-known verse that we have been considering about praying in the will of God there is a clear reference to faith:

And this is the confidence [and what is that but faith] which we have in Him, that if we ask anything according to His will He hears us. And if we know that He hears us [this too must be faith] in whatever we ask, we know that we have obtained the requests made of Him (1 John 5:14, 15).

Earlier in this same epistle John had cleared the ground over this question of faith by showing the importance of having a clear conscience if we are to approach God with assurance.

Beloved, if our hearts do not condemn us, we have confidence before God; and we receive

from Him whatever we ask, because we keep
His commandments and do what pleases Him
(1 John 3:21, 22).

There is nothing more destructive of faith than
a guilt complex or a heart that condemns us, as
John calls it. The blood of Christ, applied by confession, is the complete answer to this condition.
Then we can draw near to God 'with our hearts
sprinkled clean from an evil conscience' (Heb.
10:22).

If our prayers are to avail faith is not simply
desirable, it is essential.

Without faith it is impossible to please Him.
For whoever would draw near to God *must*
believe that He exists and that He rewards those
who seek Him (Heb. 11:6).

So faith is a 'must' if our prayers are to be pleasing to God. James stresses the same point in connection with asking God for wisdom. If we ask
for this He will give liberally provided we 'ask
in faith', but the doubter or the double-minded
man need not expect to receive anything from
the Lord (James 1:5–8). His wavering faith dis-
qualifies him from receiving the answer to a petition which would otherwise have been acceptable
to God.

Sometimes our unbelief is revealed by the timid,
half-hearted, almost apologetic way in which we
approach God. We are like the man who almost
puts a 'No' in his friend's mouth when he asks

him, 'I suppose you wouldn't be willing by any chance to let me have so and so?' Certainly when we come to God in such a spirit we are inviting His refusal, for our attitude is a denial of our standing in Christ as sons of God and of our access through Him to God. 'In whom we have boldness and confidence of access through our faith in Him' (Eph. 3 : 12 cp. Heb. 4 : 16, 10 : 19).

Sometimes our lack of faith is uncovered by a delayed answer. God keeps us waiting, and our faith which ought to be strengthened by this testing begins to fade and wither. Either we give up praying altogether or we pray on without any real confidence. At other times we continue steadfastly in prayer, despite the waiting time, until something happens which seems to knock the bottom out of our hopes. Casting away our confidence we conclude too readily that we must have been mistaken, and so the debris of another unanswered prayer is swept into the rubbish bin of 'Couldn't have been the will of God'. This is not God's way.

> Therefore do not throw away your confidence, which has a great reward. For you have need of endurance, so that you may do the will of God and receive what is promised (Heb. 10 : 35, 36).

So many of these exhortations of Scripture sound so simple, and yet in practice we find them so difficult. We readily acknowledge that we must have this boldness in approaching God, this confidence that He hears us, and this faith to hold on for the answer. But how? Once again heaven answers, 'the Holy Spirit'. Just as certainly as we recognize and confess that this lack of faith is a weakness in prayer, so we stand on the promise, 'The Spirit helps us in our weakness; for we do not know how to pray [in faith] as we ought, but the Spirit Himself intercedes for us [in faith].'

Think for a moment of that time before you knew Christ. Whether you were thoroughly godless, or whether you had a form of godliness which denied the power, you were in a state of unbelief. Then, by a gradual process or a sudden crisis, a change took place. Christ was revealed to you in a new way, and you came to see your need of Him. In some mysterious way faith was born in your heart and you became a child of God. What happened? You were born of the Spirit, for regeneration is His special work (John 3:5–8; Titus 3:5). He convicts of sin; He reveals Christ; and He creates faith in what was until then an unbelieving heart.

We may not know how the Spirit creates faith, it is enough to know that He does. Faith is one of His gifts, even as faithfulness is part of His fruit. Stephen and Barnabas were men 'full of faith and the Holy Spirit.' I take this to mean that they had a special manifestation of faith as a result of the Spirit's fullness.

We find that Scripture and experience confirm that revelation and faith are closely connected. 'Who has *believed* . . .? And to whom has the arm of the Lord been *revealed*?' (Isa. 53:1). These two questions are really one. Those who believed the report concerning Christ are those to whom Christ (the arm of the Lord) has been revealed. There is no faith without revelation. As at conversion, so throughout the Christian life, impartation of faith, strengthening of faith, increase of faith involve a continuing work of revelation.

The Holy Spirit is the great Revealer. His task is to teach us all things, as Jesus promised, but He does this by revelation, illumination and enlightenment. So Paul prayed for the Ephesians, 'that the God of our Lord Jesus Christ ... may give you a spirit of wisdom and of revelation in the knowledge of Him, having the eyes of your hearts enlightened' (1 : 17, 18). Just as it is man's heart that is enlightened, so it is man's heart that believes (Rom. 10 : 10).

Often the Holy Spirit will give us revelation on the word of God. We may have read a certain promise in the Bible time and again, but one day it lights up. The Spirit of God has given us revelation or enlightenment, and simultaneously faith is born in our hearts for the fulfilment of that promise. 'So faith comes from what is heard' (Rom. 10 : 17), but only through the operation of the Holy Spirit.

All this is deeply relevant to praying in faith. As we seek the Lord we may count on the Holy Spirit giving us revelation, and so imparting faith. He may make Bible promises to come alive, relating them to the situations for which we are interceding. Or apart from any Scripture He may simply give us revelation about those situations, so that we see them from the divine rather than the human standpoint. A conviction is born within us that God will work in that matter, though the prospect of His doing so may appear to our natural minds remote, if not impossible. That is how the possibility of the Flood must have seemed to those to whom Noah preached. That is how the birth of a baby boy promised to the aged and barren couple, Abraham and Sarah, must have appeared to their contemporaries. But these Old Testament saints believed God with a faith inspired by the Holy Spirit, and the impossible was fulfilled. Let us trust ourselves to this faith-creating Spirit. He is waiting to help us in our weakness by praying through us in living faith.

## 9

# CONTENDING WITH CIRCUMSTANCES

In a book mainly concerned with the spiritual principles of intercession there is a tendency to overlook some of the practical problems. It all sounds so easy until we come to put the thing into practice; then we meet a hundred and one difficulties and discouragements which the textbooks don't seem to mention, and soon our new enthusiasm has evaporated and we find ourselves back to 'square one'.

In these three chapters we want to anticipate some of these, for it is certain that we have all been affected by some of them at least. The point we want to emphasize is that the same Holy Spirit, whom we have seen is able to take care of the spiritual problems, can be counted on to do the same for the practical problems. He not only works positively to give us the guidance and strength we need in this ministry but also in enabling us to combat the many hindrances and discouragements we shall certainly meet. When we consider that He comes to work in us all that Christ has done for us, it is not surprising to discover that He is essentially a practical Holy Spirit.

The fact that we are so susceptible to these discouragements constitutes another aspect of our weakness in prayer, so that the same promise that

He helps us in our weakness applies here. The difficulties we have in mind proceed mainly from three sources. In this chapter we shall think of those produced by our circumstances. In the next those that are bound up with our physical weakness. And finally those that are satanic in origin.

Now there are circumstances over which we have no control which may combine to hamper our prayer life, if not to render it largely ineffective. There are the interruptions, the unexpected visitors, the telephone calls, the demands of the family. There may be a general lack of quiet, or the pressure of work that either keeps us out of the secret place or haunts us while we are there. All these and many more can be most distracting and frustrating to the would-be intercessor.

'May not these be the work of Satan?' someone is sure to ask. It is true that Satan may be responsible for a good deal of the vexing and harassing of the saints. But this is not the important question. What we need to know is, 'Is this thing the will of God for me?' It is unsound reasoning that says: 'This thing is hindering my prayer life, therefore it is of Satan and it is not the will of God for me to put up with it.' This fails to take account of the fact that many things that are the work of Satan are also equally the will of God. We only need to mention the greatest example of all—the cross. It was both the work of wicked men inspired by Satan and also the will of God. This was why Jesus did not fight against the cross but bowed His head in submission to it, though He knew that Satan was behind it (John 14:30).

Already Jesus had taught His disciples, 'Do not resist one who is evil. But if any one strikes you on the right cheek, turn to him the other also.' (Matt. 5:39). The slap on the cheek may well be inspired by Satan, but that is not a reason for resisting. God has willed this, therefore we submit to it in the confidence that it will be for His glory and for our good. There can be serious misunderstanding here due to believers having an unhealthy over-emphasis on the power and working of Satan. We ask the wrong questions and therefore arrive at the wrong conclusions. There are so many situations in which we need to see, not the working of Satan, even though he may be actively involved, but the hand of God. We should not be asking, 'What is Satan doing here?' but, 'What is God saying here?'

I find it difficult to determine which are in the more dangerous position, the majority who seem to be blind to the activity of Satan and almost completely ignorant of his devices, or that small minority of 'experts' who have become much too devil-conscious and demon-conscious, and discern satanic overtones in almost every untoward event. This is not the New Testament emphasis any more than the other. Because there are certain occasions when we may rightly resist the devil's attacks, whether through our circumstances or some other way, and experience the Lord's deliverance, we are not to assume that this is so with every case. This can mean resisting things which are the ordering of our Heavenly Father, permitted for our good, and in so doing we only succeed in frustrating both ourselves and God's purpose in that trial.

In the book of Job we are given in the first two chapters a peep behind the scenes, so we know who was responsible for the sufferings he endured. Yet it never occurred to Job or his friends to ask, 'Are these calamities the work of Satan?' Nor is there any further mention of him in the debate that followed, not even by the Almighty when He intervened. Both Job and his friends were agreed on this, if on nothing else, that these things were from the hand of God. God was speaking through these afflictions, and the moment Job got the message he was 'through', and God turned his captivity.

If we have some clear revelation or conviction that the circumstances are purely the product of Satan's malice, and therefore to be resisted, we shall of course follow this leading, and the confirmation will be the subsequent removal of the difficulty. More about this in the chapter, 'When Satan attacks'. In the absence of any such conviction we are right to take our circumstances as the providential ordering of our Heavenly Father, proving that 'in acceptance lieth peace', as Amy Carmichael expressed it.

Immediately following the remarkable scripture which is the main theme of this book, Romans 8:26 and 27, Paul reminds us that all things work together for good to those who love God (verse 28). This is a verse that we find easier to quote than to believe. Too many of us have it by rote, but not by revelation. We rebel against the providences of God. We resist the hand that afflicts us in love. Vexation and frustration are the inevitable result.

Once again the Holy Spirit is available to help us in our weakness, and that along two lines. Firstly He gives us a revelation of a sovereign God who is working all things after the counsel of His will, overruling the schemings and workings of Satan to accomplish His purpose, making the wrath of man to praise Him, and causing all things to work together for our good. The revelation that there is a divine purpose in those very things that have hindered and discouraged us in prayer, will transfigure them before our eyes.

Then He works in us a spirit of submission, so that we accept these divine orderings instead of kicking against the goad. But this is not a passive, fatalistic attitude, the 'kismet' of the Moslem— 'God wills it, therefore I accept it.' It is that acquiescence which is the product of an active faith that my very problems will be made the stepping-stones to success. It is not simply that God works all things together—the Moslem and the Hindu believe that—but that He works them together *for good*. Through facing and conquering these very difficulties we had thought were insurmountable, the Holy Spirit will work in us grace and grit, faith and fortitude, patience and perseverance—in fact the very qualities that are needed to make us real intercessors. Glory to God!

## IN WEAKNESS AND WEARINESS

WE must now deal with some practical difficulties
in the physical realm. If we are suffering from
physical or mental fatigue we may find ourselves
battling with drowsiness, wandering thoughts,
heaviness of spirit and even depression. Here it is
necessary to exercise a little discrimination. There
is a tiredness that is quite legitimate in the Christian
life. Even our Lord Himself was on one occasion
wearied with His journey, and on another He fell
asleep in the boat. When we know the Lord wants
us to fight and overcome this tiredness we have
that wonderful promise of Romans 8:11, 'He who
raised Christ Jesus from the dead will give life to
your mortal bodies also through His Spirit which
dwells in you.' Though this refers primarily to the
resurrection of our bodies, it certainly has a
present application as many have proved. The
Holy Spirit is able now to renew our weak or tired
bodies so that we may do the will of God.

When Jesus sat down by the well He was
'wearied . . . with His journey', and no doubt
hungry too. But when the disciples returned with
food and found Him busy telling the Samaritan
woman of the water of life, He appeared to have
forgotten all about His weariness, nor was He interested in food. 'I have food to eat of which you

do not know' (John 4:32). His body had been re-
newed by the Spirit of God dwelling in Him.

I well remember the first mission I conducted
after God blessed me in the Holy Spirit. A week
had passed with some measure of blessing. God
was beginning to stir the hearts of His people and
there was a widespread desire for a prolonged
time of prayer following the Sunday evening service. Tired after a full day, and with a slight headache, I wondered just how much more I could take.
By 11 p.m. there were seven of us left, almost all
young men. The time that followed till we reluc-
tantly ended at 3.30 a.m. was probably the most
remarkable season of corporate intercession I have
ever experienced. It proceeded with barely a
moment's intermission for more than four hours.
When we rose from our knees my headache had
gone, and I felt as fresh as the proverbial daisy.
The others appeared to be the same. The Holy
Spirit had given life to our mortal bodies.

There is also a state of perpetual weariness
which is unjustified, in fact dangerous, for it puts
a weapon into our enemy's hand with which to
attack us. It is a sure indication that we have got
our priorities wrong, and sooner or later the most
important things will be neglected. This situation
usually indicates that we are being ruled, even in
spiritual matters, by personal preferences, by
carnal desires, by a concern to please men—even
fellow-believers—rather than God, by an enthusiasm which results in taking on what God has
not appointed for us.

The solution is to seek the Lord with real determination until the matter is sorted out. In this we may count upon the Spirit's guidance and help. In fact we shall need all the help that He can give, for this readjustment of our priorities is neither easy to effect, nor easy to maintain, but His grace is sufficient. Unless we do this the enemy will not find it difficult to neutralize our prayer life.

Sickness of body may have much the same effect on our times with God as weariness of body. There is, of course, sickness which is a direct attack of Satan to put us out of commission if possible, and this is no more to be taken lying down than is a temptation to evil. Again, we must reserve this till the next chapter. Not all sickness, however, is in this category. Even though Satan may have a finger in it, we need to know whether or not God has a purpose in it. We have already seen that the important thing about Job's sufferings, including his physical affliction, was not that it was perpetrated by Satan but that it was permitted by God, and was for the purifying of Job's character. Very often sickness, whatever may be its direct cause, is God trying to get our ear. In that case we need to be quiet and listen to what He is trying to say to us.

On earth they say : 'Laid aside by illness';
In heaven they say : 'Called aside for stillness.'

A book on prayer is not the place to enter into discussion on the many problems that cluster around this ministry of healing, and in particular the mystery of why sickness seems to have dogged the steps of some of the Lord's choicest saints. That such cases are exceptional I do not doubt, and it is generally the will of God for His saints, as it was the prayer of the apostle John for his friend Gaius, that health of body should go hand in hand with prosperity of soul (3 John 2).

Though I have known the Lord's healing touch on more than one occasion, and believe that this ministry is for today, I cannot assert or imply, as some do, that these suffering saints were culpable in their lack of faith for healing, that they missed God's best, etc. The ready answers that are so often produced do not seem to me to be answers; they leave the mystery unravelled. Most of these great saints triumphed over their sicknesses. They did not lie down under them in defeat and self-pity. It is surely significant that Hebrews 11 not only records the faith of those who 'escaped the edge of the sword' (verse 34) but also the faith of those who were 'killed with the sword' (verse 37). Which glorified God the more—the faith of those who escaped or the faith of those who endured?

One fact is clear. Many of these saints who suffered in this way were mighty intercessors. Rightly or wrongly they accepted their afflictions as the providential ordering of the Lord. They counted on the help of the indwelling Spirit in their bodily weakness. One could make mention of Frances Ridley Havergal, Praying Hyde of India, David Brainerd of the American Indians or Robert Murray M'Cheyne of Dundee. All of these died prematurely, humanly speaking, suffering most of their lives from indifferent health, brought on by their labours for the kingdom of God. The lesson that we can surely learn from their lives is in the way they were so marvellously sustained and strengthened to prevail with God. In the midst of weakness or weariness we too may count upon the Holy Spirit coming to our aid.

## II

## WHEN SATAN ATTACKS

THE deeper one is led into this ministry of intercession the more conscious one becomes that it is
essentially a warfare in the Spirit. Before exhort-
ing the Ephesians to pray at all times in the Spirit
Paul reminds them of the true nature of this con-
flict, that it is not 'against flesh and blood, but
against the principalities, against the powers,
against the world rulers of this present darkness,
against the spiritual hosts of wickedness in the
heavenly places', and so he exhorts them to put on
the whole armour of God.

Our Lord pictures the intercessor as a widow
with a lawsuit, wearying the judge with her in-
cessant plea, 'Vindicate me against my adversary'
(Luke 18:3). Yes, our adversary the devil is ever
present, and no one is more conscious of this than
the intercessor who stands in the front line. In
this chapter we are to consider those attacks of
Satan which are designed to hinder or even nullify
the believer's intercession. We are concerned here
with those situations which are not the will of
God for us in the sense of demanding our willing
submission, but which we are to resist. Such
attacks may be made on our spirits, our minds or
our bodies.

Sometimes we may be oppressed by Satan with

a strange heaviness of spirit, which is not caused by any weariness of mind or body, nor is it the usual type of depression. With others I was once engaged in a fierce battle to free someone who was demon possessed. We decided to break off that night and resume in the morning. When I awoke I felt as though a dark cloud was enveloping me. I am not, thank God, normally subject to bouts of depression, and for a moment I was at a loss to account for my state of mind. As soon as I recalled the battle of the previous day and remembered that it was about to be resumed I realized from where the depression came. It was Satan's counter-attack to try to put me out of commission. I jumped out of bed and fell on my knees resisting and rebuking in the name of the Lord. I did not at this point address the Lord or ask for His help. I addressed Satan, using the authority the Lord had given me, and in the power of the Spirit told him to quit. Immediately the cloud lifted, and later that morning the Lord gave us the victory in prayer for the one in need. It was the Spirit who came to the rescue, giving revelation first as to the real situation, and then authority in resisting the enemy.

Sometimes we are attacked by uncertainty or perplexity. This may be especially the case when we are called by the Lord to walk with Him in the dark, not knowing quite where we are going in the path of intercession, and wondering what, if anything, is being accomplished by it all. As we do look to Jesus the Holy Spirit is free to minister to us His consolation, comfort and strength.

The prophet Zechariah was shown Joshua the high priest standing before the angel of the Lord, and Satan standing at his right hand to accuse him (Zech. 3 : 1). Now Joshua's ministry was to represent the people of God in the sanctuary which of course involved intercession. In this he was a type of our great High Priest who ever lives to make intercession for us. Because of the devastating effect upon his kingdom of such a ministry Satan is obliged to resist it with might and main. One way he does this is by accusing the brethren before God, hence his place at the right hand of Joshua.

Job was another who exercised a priestly and intercessory ministry (Job 1 : 5) and was similarly accused (Job 1 : 9–11; 2 : 4, 5). We learn from Revelation 12 : 10 that these accusations go on day and night. Often the devil makes the intercessor aware of his accusations, to bring on him a spirit of self-condemnation. We cannot approach the throne with boldness, as we are exhorted to do, if we are heeding a little voice that whispers, 'You know very well you are not fit to be interceding. What about this, that and the other?' Here is a direct attack by Satan which must be resisted.

In the case of Joshua the high priest we see that the Lord rebuked Satan, and we may rebuke him too in the Lord's name. Has he not given us authority to tread on serpents and scorpions, and over all the power of the enemy (Luke 10 : 19)? Those filthy garments—the ground of Satan's accusations—were removed from Joshua, and the Lord said, 'I have taken your iniquity away from you, and I will clothe you with rich apparel' (Zech.

3 : 4). The answer to Satan's accusations is the blood of Christ, that cleanses us from all sin, and the clothing with His righteousness.

All this is borne out by Revelation 12 : 11 to which we have already referred. There we see the saints overcoming the accuser 'by the blood of the Lamb and by the word of their testimony'. In other words, they bore witness to the blood. In this the Holy Spirit has a vital part to play, for the believer never witnesses apart from the Spirit (John 15 : 26, 27; Acts 5 : 32), and the Spirit answers to the blood. We could have no sense of a cleansed conscience or of acceptance with God apart from the witness of the Spirit. Speaking of the water and the blood John says. 'And the Spirit is the witness, because the Spirit is the truth' (1 John 5 : 6, 7). Weak and failing as we are, and so susceptible to these attacks of Satan, we can praise God that the Spirit helps us in our weakness.

Finally, as we have already indicated. Satan may be permitted to attack our bodies with sickness, and so render any concentrated intercession difficult, if not impossible. We have to recognize that such an attack is permitted by God—Satan cannot raise his little finger without first God permits it— but equally that it is the will of God that we resist it. As soon as we take up a position of faith and use our spiritual weapons in the power of the Spirit the attack will quickly pass. We have examples of this in the ministry of our Lord when He rebuked the fever that had laid low Simon's mother-in-law, and when He rebuked the storm on the lake that threatened the lives of Himself and His disciples.

The fact that He 'rebuked' suggests that there were satanic forces operating in both cases.

In these situations it is the Holy Spirit who gives us revelation and conviction as to the true nature of the attack. It is He who also gives us faith and authority to obey the scriptural injunction, 'Resist the devil and he will flee from you' (James 4:7).

## 12

## HOLDING ON

'STAYING power' in prayer is a rare quality. Our Lord realized this, and so gave at least two parables to encourage us to persevere (Luke 11 : 5–8; 18 : 1–8). There is no realm of the Christian life in which we weary so quickly as in prayer. Like Moses on the mount, our hands hang down and our knees become feeble. The reason is that persevering prayer requires a pure faith, and so often our faith is the sort that too easily rests on the visible and the outward. If there are encouraging signs to the natural eye our faith seems strong; but when, as with the story of the shipwreck in the book of Acts, neither sun nor stars appear for many days, we tend to abandon hope. It is not so much that a trial like this weakens our faith, it simply uncovers the true state of our hearts and shows us how weak our faith really is; that we are not truly walking by faith at all, but walking by sight.

The problem of holding on is chiefly the problem of learning to walk in the dark. It is hard to persevere day after day in the path of intercession, when you don't know whether anything is being accomplished by it, or whether you are any nearer your goal. If only we could see into 'the unseen'. If only we could be sure that something is happening. It is just here that the Spirit comes to our aid.

We are weak because we are in the dark, but 'the Spirit helps us in our weakness'. Are we getting tired of the refrain? It ought to be music to our souls. The spirit comes to lighten our darkness, causing us to see where we would not otherwise see and to know what we could not otherwise know.

It is not that the Spirit necessarily gives us at such times visible or tangible tokens of the Lord's working, although these will be granted from time to time. He lightens our darkness in the unseem realm. It is here we begin to see. We still have to walk by faith, but we learn that, contrary to the popular saying, 'believing is seeing'. This is of the very essence of faith. It was the secret of Moses' staying power in a day of darkness and disappoint-ment. 'He endured as seeing Him who is invisible' (Heb. 11 : 27). Every intercessor has to learn to en-dure because he is dealing with what is invisible to the natural eye. The Holy Spirit will not tell us everything that is happening or give us the answer to all our questions, but He will show us all that we need to see and tell us all that we need to know for the strengthening of our faith and to enable us to hold on.

To the weary traveller the sight of another mile-stone is an encouragement. The Spirit of God may show us, as we pray, that we have reached another milestone on the way. At times He may shed light on the situation, so that we get a glimpse of what God is doing. Or He may permit us to see in ad-vance the end of the road, so that we view the situation as it will be when our prayers are fully

answered. By such tokens the Spirit strengthens us
to persevere.

We see all this in the case of Abraham. After he
had received the promise of a son, during the waiting years that followed, God from time to time revealed Himself to the patriarch. Each time He
showed him a little more of His plan, and gave him
glimpses of the goal that lay ahead. These more
than offset the physical facts that stared him in the
face—that, as far as reproductive powers were
concerned, at a hundred years old he was 'as good
as dead', and that 'it had ceased to be with Sarah
after the manner of women'.

> In hope he believed against hope . . . He did not
> weaken in faith when he considered his own
> body . . . or the barrenness of Sarah's womb. No
> distrust made him waver concerning the promise
> of God, but he grew strong in his faith as he gave
> glory to God, fully convinced that God was able
> to do what He had promised (Rom. 4 : 18–21).

With the eye of faith Abraham could see himself holding that baby in his arms, so real had God
made that promise to him. This is the work of the
Spirit, and we may confidently expect Him to sustain us in the same way.

The Holy Spirit will often give an intercessor a
great burden, in relation to some need, from which
he can only obtain relief in intercession. It is not
uncommon for this to be the case in times preceding a visitation of the Holy Spirit. With the burden the Spirit also gives the supernatural strength

to sustain it. In this way the problem of 'holding on' is solved.

A Christian mother needs no fervent exhortation to pray without ceasing for her only child who is dangerously ill. However fitful her prayer life normally is, now she sighs her heart out in prayer all day long. There is no problem of perseverance here; the burden resting on her has solved that. Of course we can explain this in terms of natural affection and maternal instinct. But the Spirit of God is able to give the intercessor a burden of prayer for needs that would not naturally or normally concern him greater than that mother is capable of bearing, even in relation to her sick child.

The same Holy Spirit, who is able to keep us at it until the work is done, may also at times bring our praying to an abrupt halt. There was a time when the sins of Israel reached 'the point of no return', and God had to say to Jeremiah, 'Do not pray for this people' (Jer. 7:16, etc.). God would not permit His servant to waste his breath or expend his energy in vain. Just as Paul and his company were 'forbidden by the Holy Spirit' to labour any further in Asia, and so a door was opened into Europe (Acts 16:6–10), so there are times when the Spirit shuts one door in prayer so that He may open another.

The knowledge that the Holy Spirit is ready to do this kind of thing is in itself a source of great encouragement to the intercessor. He is made aware that even when he is treading the darkest path there is with him an unseen guiding hand.

Similarly, the Holy Spirit will cause him to know that his prayer is heard, that he has prevailed with God, even when there is no outward token of it, only the lifting of the burden and the welling up within him of praise. He needs no outward confirmation—that will come later—he knows by the Spirit that heaven has added its 'Amen'.

In Psalm 6 we find David labouring in prayer, with a heavy troubled spirit, as he prays for deliverance from his enemies. Then the tone of the Psalm alters abruptly (verse 8): 'Depart from me, all you workers of evil; for the Lord has heard the sound of my weeping. The Lord has heard my supplication; the Lord accepts my prayer.' He is confident that he has prevailed with God, although the outward fulfilment as far as his enemies are concerned is still future, for he concludes, 'All my enemies *shall* be ashamed and sore troubled; they *shall* turn back, and be put to shame in a moment.'

Another fine example of 'praying through' is the case of Hannah. In her great longing for a child we find her in the temple fasting, weeping, praying and making her vows to God. When Eli said to her, 'Go in peace, and the God of Israel grant your petition' (1 Sam. 1 : 17) the Spirit registered within her that her cry was heard; her burden of sorrow was lifted, and she went away with a deep peace and assurance in her heart. I am sure that she never asked God again. She knew that she had prevailed.

So much for the various ways in which the Holy Spirit helps us in our weakness. We must now return to Ephesians 6 : 18 where we are exhorted to pray in the Spirit 'with all prayer and supplication', that is, with *all kinds of prayer* and supplication. In the next chapters we are to deal with the three kinds of praying in the Spirit referred to earlier: praying with the mind, praying with the spirit and praying without words, all of which are taught in the New Testament.

## 13

## WITH WORDS UNDERSTOOD

WHEN we 'pray with the mind', as Paul expresses it, we must of necessity use words that we understand, even though the prayer may be inaudible. In the next chapter we shall speak of the second kind of praying in the Spirit, with words that are unknown. For the moment we are concerned to know how the Holy Spirit girds our minds and guides our thinking as we pray with our understanding.

We have no right to expect a special leading of the Spirit here, if we are not submitting to His leading in other realms. In Romans 8, where we find the theme verse of this book, Paul reminds us that the leading of the Spirit is a mark of sonship (verse 14). The leading of the Spirit in the realm of prayer is nothing more than a development of this general principle.

Paul speaks at the commencement of that same chapter of what God has done to free us from the domination of the flesh (verse 3). Walking according to the Spirit is contrasted with walking according to the flesh. Walking according to the Spirit is basic to praying in the Spirit. We must have the waters to the ankles before we can know waters to the knees (Ezek. 47:3, 4). Can we really conceive of someone who walks after the flesh and yet prays in the Spirit? Can carnal living and spiritual praying go together? Whatever spiritual praying this is, it is not the New Testament variety, the product of an ungrieved Holy Spirit. It is foolish to expect to be led into these deeper realms of Spirit-led intercession, if we are not submissive to our Guide in the practical issues of daily life. An uncondemned heart is essential (1 John 3:21, 22). As we move on in the path of intercession we shall find that the Holy Spirit will require more implicit obedience, and greater sensitivity to His will.

The matter of the Holy Spirit directing our thoughts in prayer takes us to the basic fact that all prayer begins in the heart of God. Matthew Henry said: 'When God intends great mercy for His people he sets them apraying.' Indeed, when God wants anything accomplished in His Kingdom He moves men to pray. God is always the initiator. All effectual prayer was moving in the heart of God before ever it began to move in the heart of man. What Kepler said as he unlocked the secrets of the starry heavens, could well be said by the man who prays in the Spirit: 'O God, I am thinking Thy thoughts after Thee.'

Some have used the electric circuit as a helpful illustration of this truth. If there is to be a flow of electricity, then there must be a source of power. In the circuit of prayer, the power supply proceeds from God, but the power itself is the Spirit who is ever proceeding from the Father (John 15:26). The intercessor is like an electric lamp wired into the circuit. God wishes to work in a certain situation, and so He moves upon a believer by His Spirit. It is God that burdens him to pray. As he yields himself his whole being becomes a willing instrument for the Spirit's activity. The spiritual current flows through him as electricity through a lamp, and his prayer returns by the Spirit back to the heart of God.

All illustrations have their limitations, and this is no exception. It helps us to see the truth about prayer originating in God and returning to God, but when it comes to such practical matters as how we can be wired into the circuit, and how our minds and wills are to be blended with the mind and will of the Spirit, it cannot help us. How may our minds be so controlled by the Spirit as we pray that we do in fact think God's thoughts after Him?

Often this will be spontaneous, almost instinctive. The mind and will of the believer is yielded to the Spirit, and the Spirit is expressing Himself through him, without his being necessarily conscious of this. When Paul speaks of being led by the Spirit (Rom. 8 : 14) the thought is not so much of a conscious apprehension of the mind of the Spirit, followed by a conscious act of obedience, but rather an instinctive action by the believer who is now animated, not by an evil spirit, not even merely by the human spirit, but by the Spirit of God. Family traits are instinctive; so that what Paul is saying is that God's family traits are apparent in the behaviour of God's sons, because they are led by God's Spirit. They are naturally spiritual, and spiritually natural (using 'natural' in its general, not its theological sense). This applies to the prayer life as much as to any other realm.

Not far from the home of a small boy lived a famous artist. The youngster heard all about this great man, and dreamed of the day when he too would paint great pictures. When the artist died the boy thought to himself, 'If only I could have one of his brushes I would paint great pictures.' He knocked at the door of the great house where the artist had lived. The lady dressed in black smiled sadly at the flushed and eager face. She brought him one of the artist's brushes, and he took it home with great excitement. It was a crestfallen little boy that later returned the brush to the lady saying that he couldn't paint any better with it than he did with his own. 'To become a great painter,' explained the lady, 'you need more than the artist's brush, you need the spirit of the artist.'

As the Spirit of our great Intercessor inspires us, we shall often pray instinctively, just as the artist is inspired by the artistic spirit within him. As far as we are concerned they are our thoughts, our petitions, our pleadings, but since we are led by the Spirit God will know that they are really those of the One who dwells within us.

There may be, however, a conscious apprehension of the Spirit's burden followed by a conscious response to it. In this case the intercessor is not so much like a lamp in the electric circuit as a radio which is both a receiver and transmitter. The receiving aspect is often quite overlooked in the ministry of intercession. Communion with God should surely be a two-way traffic. We speak of prayer as our 'coming to the mercy seat', but when God first spoke about this to Moses He said nothing about it as a place where Moses would speak with Him, but rather as a place where He would speak with Moses (Exod. 25:22). In other words, the mercy seat was to be first a place of revelation, and then a place of intercession.

This revelation may indeed be given to the intercessor as he prays, but it will often be necessary to tune in and hear what heaven is saying that he may know how to pray. To learn how to talk to God we must first learn how to listen to God. 'Let every man be quick to hear, slow to speak' (James 1:19) was said about our converse with one another, but we would do well to apply it also to converse with God. How often we rush thoughtlessly into God's presence and blurt out our requests. No human subject would behave like this in audience with his sovereign or head of state. How fitting are Solomon's words here:

> Guard your steps when you go to the house of God; to draw near to listen is better than to offer the sacrifice of fools; for they do not know that they are doing evil. Be not rash with your mouth, nor let your heart be hasty to utter a word before God, for God is in heaven, and you upon earth; therefore let your words be few (Eccl. 5:1, 2).

Many believers today when they read, 'The word of the Lord came to Elijah', or 'The Lord said to Samuel', assume that this was some audible voice, and that God does not speak to men nowadays, since He has spoken once for all in His Son and in

His written word. Although God did occasionally speak to men in an audible voice, I am sure that in most cases it was the inner voice that God used. It is certain that He still most often uses this means, though one has heard of rare cases of an audible voice being heard today. It is essential that we seek God's face and train ourselves to listen.

In my early days as a soldier in the Armoured Corps we were trained in wireless telegraphy. We were sent out in army trucks over Salisbury Plain, each having its own transmitter, and we had to maintain a radio link with the control station at base. From time to time control would send out a tuning call, and we had to check our receiver. If the receiver was tuned in, then the transmitter was automatically tuned in. So often our spiritual receiving sets have never been tuned, and so our transmissions are 'way out', and 'Control' never hears us.

This tuning in to heaven involves the lost art of *waiting on God*. David had learned how to do this, for he says in Psalm 62 : 1 (R.V.), 'My soul waiteth only upon God' (Heb. 'is silent unto God'; cp. verse 5). There is a waiting on God that involves being silent in God's presence; in other words, listening. God will speak to us by His Spirit, and when He has spoken we shall know how to pray.

The ways in which the Holy Spirit speaks will vary with different individuals, and may even vary with the same individual on different occasions. It may be an impression or a burden in one's spirit. He may stimulate our memories and bring back to us some incident or some need. He may speak in the quietness of our hearts or illumine some Scripture to us. He may enlighten our minds concerning some matter for which He would have us intercede. Let us expect Him to do it. Let us give Him opportunity to do it. Let us yield our minds to the Spirit that our praying may be the expression of His mind. But remember, we shall need to exercise faith. Having yielded our minds we must resist that whisper, 'It's just you making it up.' We must trust ourselves to the Spirit of truth, believing that we are indeed receiving His message, His burden, His impression, and the confirmation will follow.

## 14

## WITH WORDS UNKNOWN

WE come now to another kind of praying in the Spirit, which Paul distinguishes from that just considered in which the mind or understanding is the vehicle of the Spirit's activity. As there has been much misunderstanding here we must read what the apostle says carefully, and then examine it in its context.

> Therefore, he who speaks in a tongue should pray for the power to interpret. For if I pray in a tongue, my spirit prays but my mind is unfruitful. What am I to do? I will pray with the spirit and I will pray with the mind also (1 Cor. 14: 13–15).

The apostle's argument in the preceding verses (6–12) is clear. Speaking in tongues in the church does not profit the hearers if they do not understand what is being said. Thus, in seeking for gifts, let your main object be the building up of the church. 'Therefore'—to return to the opening verse of our passage—'he who speaks in a tongue should pray for the power to interpret' (verse 13). So Paul is here making a plea for the exercise of interpretation of tongues, which the Corinthians were evidently neglecting. It is the public use of tongues that Paul is dealing with here. Unless we are clear on this point we shall misunderstand what immediately follows.

Paul goes on to explain that when he prays in tongues he is praying with his spirit, but not with his mind (verse 14). His mind is unfruitful since he does not understand the language. This, of course, is true for the minds of his hearers; since they do not understand either, they are not edified. Now he is in a quandary, for if God has given him this gift then surely it is to be used. 'What am I to do?' he asks himself. The answer is in this gift of interpretation which he is here emphasizing. So he continues:

I will pray with the spirit [that is, in a tongue] and I will pray with the mind also [that is, giving the interpretation of the tongue].

Paul had said earlier (verse 2) that speaking in tongues (whether in public or in private) was primarily a speaking unto God and not to man; that is, it took the form of prayer rather than exhortation. Now we learn that the interpretation of a tongue may also be in the form of inspired prayer or thanksgiving, rather than a prophetic utterance to the people.

Having spoken of praying with the spirit followed by praying with the understanding, of singing with the spirit followed by singing with the understanding, he adds, by way of explanation:

Otherwise, if you bless with the spirit [that is,

give thanks in a tongue—without also blessing with the understanding] how can anyone in the position of an outsider say the 'Amen' to your thanksgiving when he does not know what you are saying?

Clearly, then, it is *in church* that Paul is contemplating this praying with the spirit, singing with the spirit and blessing with the spirit. Otherwise there would be no question of the outsider being able, or unable to add his 'Amen'. Until we reach verse 18 it is not clear whether Paul personally prayed in tongues. 'If I pray in tongues' and 'I will pray with the spirit', etc., could be hypothetical. But now he goes on to say:

I thank God that I speak in tongues more than you all; nevertheless, in church I would rather speak five words with my mind, in order to instruct others, than ten thousand words in a tongue (verses 18 and 19).

It is important to take these two verses together. In one breath he says that he spoke in tongues more than any of the Corinthians—and that was certainly saying something!—and in the next breath that *in church* he would prefer to speak five words with his mind, in order to instruct others, than ten thousand words in a tongue. We cannot escape from the clear statement of verse 18, that Paul used the gift of tongues extensively, but hastening to add, 'nevertheless, in church I would rather . . .' implies that his extensive use of the gift was *not* in church. This is not to say that he never used it in church, or that it was wrong to use it in church, provided there was interpretation (verses 13–17). Presumably it was because God had equipped him with other and greater gifts 'in order to instruct others' (verse 19) which he generally preferred to use.

If then Paul spoke so much in tongues, but did not do so in church, where did he exercise this gift? The answer can only be, in his private devotions. Without a doubt praying and giving thanks with the spirit (i.e. in tongues) played a very important part in the devotional life of this great apostle. Far from disparaging it, as some do, Paul gave thanks to God for the extensive use he was able to make of it. We too must be careful not to disparage it if only for this reason that it is a precious gift of God.

As we have already said Paul was discussing the use of this gift in church, for that was where things had gone wrong at Corinth, but he himself testifies to the use of it out of church. It was an invaluable tool in his devotional kit, a powerful weapon in his spiritual armoury, and it is this aspect that concerns us here. If he could refer to praying with the spirit, singing with the spirit, and blessing with the spirit *in church*, then it is certain that these were rightful uses of the gift in the privacy of one's own devotions. Some have been quick to point out how limited was the use of this gift in public, according to Paul; but from this very teaching we can learn how unlimited was its use in private.

The devotional use of this gift, and particularly its use in the ministry of intercession, takes us right back to the commencement of this chapter of 1 Corinthians where the apostle says, 'For one who speaks in a tongue speaks not to men but to God' (14:2). This was even true at Pentecost. The tongues then was not a preaching of the gospel in other languages—this Peter did later and was understood in his mother tongue—but was a declaration of the mighty works of God (Acts 2:11), presumably an ascription of praise to God in similar vein to what we have in Psalms 135 and 136. The manifestation in the house of Cornelius was similarly described as 'extolling God' (Acts 10:46) which Peter later referred to as 'the same gift ... as He gave to us' on the day of Pentecost (Acts 11:17). It is clear, then, that the primary use of tongues is Godward, not manward.

Though our main emphasis is intercession, a word may not be out of place here on the use of tongues in praise and thanksgiving. 'If you bless with the spirit ... you may give thanks well enough' (verses 16, 17). Paul's restricting of the gift here is because of the presence of 'the other man' who is not helped by an utterance he does not understand. In the solitude of one's own devotions these restrictions no longer apply. Only God is present, and 'one who speaks in tongues speaks not to men but to God' (verse 2).

But is it not better to do it in your mother tongue and understand what you are saying? Not necessarily, or God would never have given this gift, nor would Paul have used it so much. Have we not known times when, in adoration of the Lord, we feel the inadequacy of our own language to express all that we feel in our hearts? The very language which is usually an indispensable channel of communication seems to become a barrier to communication. It is then that this gift comes to our aid, and the human spirit is released in an utterance of praise or thanksgiving that would not have been possible in our native tongue. We are not necessarily speaking of ecstasy but simply of liberty in the Spirit. The use of the expression 'ecstatic gift' in referring to tongues is a misnomer. One is not required to be in an ecstatic state to exercise this gift.

There is also an experience of personal edification in the exercise of this gift, as Paul explains in verse 4. This is not difficult to understand when we remember that edification is not primarily a thing of the human mind but of the human spirit. The Holy Spirit can bypass our minds and minister direct to our spirits. Have we never had an uplift by simply a sense of the Lord's presence? To those who find all this somewhat mystifying we would say, the experience is not nearly so difficult as the explanation!

In the realm of intercession we should look on tongues as another weapon in our armoury. We may pray more generally with our understanding, yet this gift has a value and importance all its own. Sometimes it is manifestly an advantage to pray in a language that you do not understand, provided of course the Holy Spirit is inspiring the language, and that is always so if one is praying in the Spirit.

We have already seen that the Holy Spirit is able to illuminate our minds when we are praying over some matter with inadequate knowledge. But there are times when we do not need to know the facts—perhaps important that we do *not* know. It is here that praying with the spirit may take over from praying with the mind, enabling us to pray beyond our knowledge of the situation, because the Holy Spirit who inspires the language knows all the facts.

We usually know at such times that our words are intercession, rather than praise or thanksgiving, and although we do not know what we are saying, it is enough to know that the Holy Spirit is inspiring it, and that the prayer will therefore be right 'on target'. What does it matter that we do not understand the words when we know that God does?

As we have pointed out earlier, praying in the Spirit is not necessarily praying in tongues, but praying in tongues should always be praying in the Spirit. It is possible for a gift that is truly of God to be operated in a fleshly way. As Paul shows in Chapter 13, if I have divine gifts without divine love, 'I am a noisy gong', 'I am nothing', 'I have nothing'—no reflection on the gift, only on me. There was nothing wrong with the gifts at Corinth, but there was a lot wrong with the Corinthians. How could they be 'carnal' or 'of the flesh' (3 : 1–3) and at the same time expect to operate their gifts in the Spirit?

To return to the matter of praying in tongues, it is not that tongues is a superior kind of prayer, just that it is another very valuable kind. Paul says 'Pray at all times in the Spirit with all [kinds of] prayer and supplication'—and this, with words unknown, is one of them. It has this added advantage over praying with the mind that the mind can relax, which is a great help when the mind is too tired for prolonged concentration. There is no suggestion here of making the mind a blank, for that can be dangerous.

An experience, some years ago, brought home to me the authority we may wield by this form of prayer, and how Satan fears it. I had assumed that James' words about the demons trembling or shuddering (James 2 : 19) referred to the abyss or some other unseen realm. I never thought that I would witness it. It was a case of demon possession. I had prayed in English, and also rebuked the enemy in the name of the Lord. This only served to stir him up, and the manifestations were fearful to behold. I was suddenly moved to rebuke the demon in tongues, a thing I had never done before. I was conscious of the authority with which the words came forth. The effect was electric. The person, by now in a kind of coma and completely under the control of the spirit, trembled from head to foot. When a little later I repeated this action the effect was the same, which assured me that this was no coincidence.

The devil knows that there is authority in the right use of this gift, but I believe he fears it, not so much because of what it is in itself, but because, manifested as it was on the day of Pentecost, it is a symbol of the power and gifts of the Spirit in this age, the weapons that God has given us to plunder the strong man's house. If demons realize this, how much more Satan and those higher orders, the principalities and powers in the heavenly realm. Perhaps this is why Satan has attacked this gift so vehemently and relentlessly, seeking to corrupt and spoil it on the one hand, and to despise and vilify it on the other.

How may this gift be received? Generally it is given through the experience of the baptism in the Spirit. Seek the Lord for the promised enduement and if there is in your heart desire and faith for this gift He will surely give it. If you have truly received the Holy Spirit in power but without tongues, then ask Him for the gift. Someone may be quick to warn us, 'Seek the Giver, not the gifts —the Person, not the power.' This may sound very spiritual, but it is not in accord with Scripture. We are to 'seek the Lord *and His strength*' (Psa. 105:4). We are to seek the Giver *and* His gifts. It is certainly wrong to seek gifts for themselves, but right to seek them because we want more of Him, and He comes to us in His gift—they are manifestations of Him. Like everything else gifts are received simply on the basis of faith. Rest your faith on God's promises. The references given at the conclusion of this chapter will be a help here.

Let us, then, use this gift as a weapon of intercession. We are exhorted to 'pray in the Spirit . . . with all [kinds of] prayer' including praying in tongues. Let us not be ashamed of being imitators of the great apostle who thanked God that he used this gift more than the Corinthians abused it. Remember, the answer to misuse is not non-use but right use.

Psa. 37:4, 84:11; Mat. 7:11 with Luke 11:13; Mark 11:24; 1 Cor. 14:1.

## 15

## WITHOUT WORDS

WE have seen that praying in the Spirit may mean praying with the native tongue, that is, 'with the mind'; or praying with the new tongue (promised in Mark 16:17), that is, 'with the spirit'. But it may also mean praying with no tongue at all, that is, 'with sighs too deep for words' (R.S.V.) or 'groanings which cannot be uttered' (A.V., R.V.). This is a very important aspect of the teaching of Romans 8:26, 27 that we must now consider.

If some have found the idea of praying in an unknown tongue perplexing, they may find this idea of inarticulate praying even more so, for here there is no language at all—the only speech is sighs and the only grammar groans, and even these are silent because inexpressible. It should be emphasized here that this type of praying is not generally for the public gathering but for the secret place.

Let us not shut our minds to what at first may appear to be incomprehensible, even irrational. Of course it is not irrational; like so much else in the realm of the Spirit it is super-rational. Faith can lead us into this realm, but not reason. Let us come, then, to this teaching of God's word with a reverent and humble spirit, and the prayer: 'Teach me what I do not see' (Job 34:32).

Notice that in this passage Paul speaks of the groaning of the whole creation (verse 22), the groaning of the believer (verse 23) and finally the 'groanings which cannot be uttered' (A.V., R.V.) of the Spirit Himself (verse 26). Since the same root word is used in this last verse (26) as in the other two verses (22 and 23)[1] we shall follow the A.V. and R.V. rendering and refer to the 'groanings' of the Spirit, rather than the 'sighs too deep for words' of the R.S.V. However, the important point is that, whichever rendering we prefer, this refers to a form of praying without words.

To many this reference to the groaning of the Spirit presents no problem. They assume that this intercession of the Holy Spirit is, like the intercession of Christ at the Father's right hand, performed quite apart from us. It has not registered with them that it has anything to do with the believer, except that it is performed on his behalf. Once we grasp the fact that the Holy Spirit never intercedes for us except He intercedes in us and through us, we begin to see the significance of the Spirit's groaning.

In an earlier chapter we referred to the change of punctuation adopted by the R.S.V. in verses 15–16: 'When we cry, "Abba! Father!" it is the Spirit Himself bearing witness with our spirit ...' When *we* cry, it is *the Spirit* crying. The action of the divine Spirit merges with that of the human spirit to produce a joint-witness. In the same way this groaning is a joint-groaning of the believer (verse 23) and the Spirit (verse 26).

Notice that we who groan are said to have 'the

first fruits of the Spirit'. Ours is therefore of a different order to the groaning of the whole creation; it is wholly spiritual because it is the product of the Spirit. We may think of the groaning as part of the first fruits—the produce of His working in us.

Note that it is the Spirit who groans, and that God has sent Him forth into our hearts. So it is *in our hearts* where His groaning takes place. 'And He who searches the hearts of men,' continues the apostle, 'knows what is the mind of the Spirit' (verse 27). In speaking of the One who searches the hearts of men he is obviously referring to God (1 Sam. 16:7; Jer. 17:10). Why, then, does he not say 'God'? Surely to impress upon us that it is the great *Searcher of human hearts* who knows what the Spirit's groaning means, for it is in human hearts that the groaning takes place. Notice also how the reference to the believer groaning 'inwardly' (verse 23) corresponds to the Spirit's 'groanings which cannot be uttered' (verse 26 R.V.).

Can we groan inwardly and not be aware of it? Can the Spirit groan within us and we not know it? Surely not, if these two groanings are one. What has been said of the other two kinds of praying in the Spirit is equally true of this. It is our praying inspired and energized by the Spirit within us. The believer is praying without words simply because that is the manner in which the Spirit is moving within him.

In the earlier chapters much truth has been drawn from these two verses in Romans 8 without any mention of this particular kind of wordless praying. That is because the basic facts of our weakness and the Spirit's help are true, whatever the kind of praying. There are principles here that can have wider application than that which Paul gives to them. This should not obscure the fact that the reference here is specifically to inarticulate praying. Since this is the only passage in the Bible which teaches us what praying in the Spirit really is, it should at least impress us with the importance of this aspect, even if it does not actually lead us to conclude that this is the highest and most powerful form of prayer available to man.

On the face of it the idea of prayer being conveyed in the form of groans or sighs rather than words is difficult. How can such convey anything to God?—we may ask. The apostle seems to anticipate this question, for he continues:

> And He who searches the hearts of men knows what is the mind of the Spirit, because the Spirit intercedes for the saints according to the will of God.

Though the prayer be but an inaudible sigh or groan deep in the heart of the intercessor, God the searcher of hearts knows what the Spirit is conveying. Here surely is what may be rightly called 'the language of the Spirit'—that which is peculiarly His own, while 'tongues' is but the language of men, or possibly angels.

Now the original does not actually say that the

Spirit intercedes 'according to the will of God', but simply 'according to God'. This is even stronger, for it suggests that the Spirit's activity is not merely in harmony with God's will but actually regulated by God. So we are back to the picture of the electric circuit—the impulse that comes from God by the Spirit returns to God.

Groaning is the expression of physical or mental suffering, and here, in the context of Romans 8, the figure that Paul uses is the pain of childbirth. In verse 22 he speaks of 'groaning in travail'. A woman in labour not only groans because of her labour pains but also with desire to bring forth. It is not just pain, but pain transfigured by longing, by hope, by expectation.

In this realm of prayer-travail described by Paul in verses 26 and 27, there is inevitably suffering, but its nature is spiritual, though it may have physical accompaniments. Naturally we shrink from this, but let the following considerations strengthen us for whatever the Spirit may demand. Firstly, this is one aspect of the 'fellowship of Christ's sufferings'. It is said of Him in the garden, 'being in an agony He prayed more earnestly; and His sweat became like great drops of blood falling down upon the ground' (Luke 22:44). He invited three disciples to share that lonely prayer vigil, but they failed Him. Shall we fail Him now in His great unfinished work of intercession?

Then there is the glorious fact which we have emphasized throughout this book, 'the Spirit helps us in our weakness'—even in this weakness we feel in the face of suffering. He comes in His capacity as the Comforter, to solace our griefs, to ease our pains, to strengthen our wills that we may not faint, nor even flinch, but endure to the end. Finally, there is the glorious hope which is the subject of the whole passage to spur us on. We are travailing to bring forth. A new age is about to be born—and how much nearer we are to it than when Paul penned these words to the Roman believers. The sons of God are to be manifested. A new 'man' is to appear before the universe in the perfection of his manhood, having come to the measure of the stature of the fullness of Christ.

We may have read the lives of great intercessors like 'Praying Hyde' of India, and perhaps we have associated this kind of praying with such. No doubt, we argue, these had a special call and a special ministry in this realm, but it is altogether beyond people like ourselves. This may provide us with an easy escape, but let us first ask ourselves whether it may not be a cover for our unwillingness or our unbelief. And before we settle for the 'specialist' theory let us read the passage again with hearts truly open to the Lord, and ask ourselves if there is any hint in Paul's words that this is a special ministry involving a special call. He says:

We ourselves, who have the first fruits of the Spirit [are you included here?], groan inwardly as we wait for adoption as sons, the redemption of our bodies. For in this hope we were saved ... But if we hope for what we do not see, we wait for it with patience. Likewise the Spirit helps us in our weakness; for we do not know how to pray as we ought, but the Spirit Himself intercedes for us with sighs too deep for words.

It would seem that Paul is speaking in very general terms, and that if we have ears to hear, hearts to receive, and wills to obey, we may trust ourselves to our Heavenly Teacher to lead us into this deep mystery of prayer. I believe that in these closing days of this age the Lord will raise up an army of intercessors who pray at all times in the Spirit, with all kinds of prayer, including this.

[1] In verses 22 and 23 the verb forms, *sunstenazo* (to groan together), and *stenazo* (to groan) are used. In verse 26 it is the noun form, *stenagmos* (a groaning).

## 16

## TRAVAIL AND TEARS

To illustrate and amplify what has been said I want, in this chapter and the one following, to call a few intercessors into the witness box. I know them each personally, and I am grateful to them for being willing to lay bare their hearts in order to share with us, anonymously of course, some of those deep and intimate things that they have experienced in the secret place—things which would not normally or generally be shared. To those who have not yet begun to move in this wonderful realm of the Spirit there may be some things here that will perplex or even offend. But we must take this risk for the sake of others in quest of a life of power with God, who will find here that 'deep calls to deep'.

Please remember that we are dealing with experiences which belong to the solitude of the prayer room. Here are words of those who have gone farther in than most, just as the Saviour in Gethsemane left His foremost apostles and went 'a little farther', where He prayed in a way that would certainly shock most Christians if it happened in the church prayer meeting—with strong crying and tears, His sweat like drops of blood, as He lay prostrate on the ground.

One thing that must surely impress the reader is

that there is both similarity and diversity in the experiences recorded here. This is one of the hallmarks of God's workmanship which we find in the physical as well as the spiritual realm. The similarity teaches us that there are principles operating here which hold good for all those who would pray in the Spirit. The diversity is a warning not to pattern our prayer life after this one or that. The Spirit will express Himself through us in His own way.

This testimony comes from a married woman with a family, whose husband is a business executive. In addition to both husband and wife being involved in evangelistic and church work, they have a very busy household to which many come for counsel and help. It has proved to be for many a meeting place with God. In the personal letter which accompanied her testimony she wrote:

I am very conscious that in disclosing these intimate spiritual experiences, even though under God's definite direction and with the knowledge that my testimony is to be anonymous, I must be meticulously careful to remind myself and you that I am nothing, have nothing and never will be anything outside of His amazing grace; and that 'of Him and through Him and to Him are all things'.

I asked this sister to share particularly her experiences of inarticulate praying, and so she has concentrated on this particular aspect.

'During times of prayer when the burden has

intensified to the point where words ceased, the Holy Spirit has used two main methods to express the burden of the Father's heart for the object of prayer. Firstly, loud involuntary regular groanings, exactly the same as when I was in labour before giving birth to my children, except that instead of the pain there were intensity of desire and deep longing in the Spirit. The mind is centred on God in an attitude of faith that He is doing something deep and permanent to bring about the requests for which I have prayed.

'I have no sudden or dramatic results to report from this form of intercession as it has only come upon me when praying for people and projects that take a long process to accomplish. It happened when praying for a vital Christian couple to go further in discipleship. Christ prayed for this in John 17, and what followed showed that the results were not immediate in the case of the disciples. I have experienced this too when praying individually for men of God to become greater men of God—more holy, more humble, more Christlike, and more effective for God. Scripture teaches that the development of the man of God takes many years to accomplish, and I am confident that, on the occasions that the Holy Spirit has travailed through me in this way, something very real has been accomplished which may not be immediately apparent. I have also known this travail when praying for an outpouring of God's Spirit upon my own nation (Isa. 66:8).

'Secondly, there have been times when a deep desire begins with words, and then goes on into intense, uncontrollable weeping as though the heart would break. This has happened when praying for lost souls over many years. On one occasion I was praying at home for prisoners in a jail at the time an evangelist was preaching the gospel to them. It lasted for about ten minutes during which time I felt within my whole being something of what it was like to be bound by their sin, their guilt, their helplessness, their despair, especially those on long term sentences. It was awful. The intense desire of the Spirit expressed through the weeping was for them to have hope and freedom through receiving Christ.

'I believe this experience in prayer prepared me as nothing else could have for the years that followed when I regularly visited these men and had the great joy of leading some of them to the Lord while they were still in the prison. One of these was on a long sentence, having committed one of the worst offences, and was greatly despised by the other prisoners. Another, on release, commenced to worship regularly with other Christians, married a fine Christian girl, and established a Christian home. I cannot describe the joy I felt at his wedding.

'When, over the years, I have been burdened to pray for those bound by the chains of sin and Satan, especially those in the grip of drug addiction, alcoholism, prostitution and sex perversion, I have known the same intense weeping and feeling of utter despair. Years later God led me into a work which reached out to such, and I have seen some of them find deliverance in Christ.

'After a day of prayer and fasting, for souls to be saved prior to an evangelistic crusade, this intense weeping came upon me as I prayed for a Jew, very influential in both religious and business circles. I had already prayed for him for two years. He came with us to the Crusade and was deeply stirred by the Holy Spirit. This was followed by a further year of intercession, after which he died suddenly, without our knowing whether or not he had found Christ. God alone knows the destiny of this man's soul. I learned much through this experience of God's pursuing love.

'Perhaps the greatest agony I have experienced for a lost soul was in circumstances which made it inexpedient for any groanings to be expressed at all. One Sunday morning the preacher announced that he would be preaching that night on the subject of hell from the story of the rich man and Lazarus, and that there might be someone in the evening service for whom it would be the last opportunity to receive Christ. He asked for special prayer. I knew at once that this referred to an unconverted friend, a business executive, to whom my husband had faithfully given the gospel on several occasions, and for whom much prayer had been made. We phoned him and he consented to come. In the afternoon as I prayed the burden of his desperate need came upon me, and words gave way to intense weeping, with a great longing that he would repent before it was too late. That evening he sat beside me throughout the service as the Holy Spirit agonized through me for his salvation. In utter silence and perfect stillness of body I ex-

perienced a travail of spirit as intense as anything
I have ever known. It seemed I could see his s
spiralling down to a lost eternity, and, as I pra
without ceasing, I sensed the force of the I
Spirit's work was gradually but surely drawing
man back. The only outward indication that a
thing was happening to me was the silent fal
of tears. He responded to the appeal, and after t
service he knelt with the preacher and myself, re-
pented of his sin and committed his life to Christ.

'I had been praying regularly for some years for
a very fine minister's only son who had professed
Christ as a boy, but who had for years been right
away from God. He had made a mess of his life,
and had been the heartbreak of his parents. One
night as I prayed for him, words ceased and prolonged uncontrollable weeping came upon me.
This greatly encouraged me to believe that God
was still striving with this young man, though so
many had been praying for him for so long with
no apparent result. Subsequent events have confirmed that God is working in him.

'When in prayer for the nation to be saved from
the judgment we so obviously deserve, pleading
God's character of long-suffering and mercy, intense and heart-breaking weeping has come upon
me, that we might be spared all that He has
planned in judgment. Only one oft-repeated word
has come from my lips with the weeping—the
word "mercy". Following the weeping has been
a feeling of physical exhaustion.

'One other experience I would record concerns
a deep purging work in my own life. God had been

dealing with me for some days over the sin of pride in several specific matters. I became concerned that there must be a considerable root of this sin in my heart for all these little branches to be showing up. So one day I shut myself in a room and asked God to show me my heart as He saw it —especially the sin of pride. Nothing happened. I prayed more earnestly, looking to Him in faith, believing that I was asking according to His will, for His glory and my good. Still nothing.

'I began to wrestle with God, told Him repeatedly that I would not let Him go, that I meant what I was saying with all my heart, and wept before Him with deep desire. Then it came, just as I had asked. I could do nothing but weep and weep as though my heart would break as I saw the awfulness of this sin in the sight of a holy God. With such a revelation, repentance was instantaneous. I knew I had to acknowledge the conviction of pride to a servant of God before whom much of it had been committed. I did, and the wonderful peace that followed more than compensated for the humbling experience of having to make confession in this way.

'In the preceding testimony I have concentrated on one particular aspect of prayer, as I was requested to do. I hope that the reader will not be left with the impression that this ministry of intercession is all tears and travail. I find that God also gives me times of great joy and exhilaration. Words cannot convey what a wonderfully varied and thrilling ministry it is.'

## 17

# THE UNPREDICTABLE HOLY SPIRIT

THERE is nothing routine about the path of the Spirit-led intercessor, and consequently he is never liable to be troubled by monotony. Labour and self-discipline there certainly is, but to this is added the spice of mystery and even excitement. The intercessor never knows what lies 'just around the corner'. He can never assume that because the Spirit led this way yesterday He will do so again today. He comes almost to expect the unexpected and to look upon the unpredictable as usual, as indeed a characteristic of the Spirit's working.

Our Lord alluded to this in speaking to Nicodemus of the regenerating work of the Holy Spirit. He said, 'The wind blows where it wills, and you hear the sound of it, but you do not know whence it comes or whither it goes' (John 3:8). 'Wind' here is the usual word for 'spirit' (or 'breath'), and elsewhere in Scripture, as we know, wind is used as a symbol for the Spirit's activity (e.g. Ezek. 37 and Acts 2). But the interesting thing about our Lord's reference to the wind is that He does not apply it directly to the Spirit—'so it is with the Spirit', but to the believer—'so it is with everyone who is born of the Spirit'. In other words, just as the wind is to us incomprehensible and unpredictable in its movements, so is the activity of one born of the Spirit.

This fact may be applied to praying in the Spirit. This unpredictable feature of the Spirit's working is reflected in the prayer life of the believer who is led of the Spirit. Of course we must never entertain the thought that the Holy Spirit is unpredictable in the sense of being unreliable—as many humans are. If His ways are incomprehensible they are certainly not irrational. There is nothing freakish or capricious about the Holy Spirit's activity. He is not subject to whim and fancy. His working will often transcend reason, but will never contradict it. That we do not know the 'whence' and the 'whither' of the Spirit's movings is simply due to our limited vision and understanding of the unseen realm.

Before that confrontation with the prophets of Baal on Mount Carmel, Elijah told Obadiah, the steward of Ahab's household, to tell his master Ahab, 'Behold, Elijah is here.' Obadiah was terrified at this suggestion :

> As soon as I have gone from you, the Spirit of the Lord will carry you whither I know not; and so, when I come and tell Ahab and he cannot find you, he will kill me.

Of course, Obadiah's fear was groundless, for the Spirit does not move a man to say one thing and then immediately act contrary to it. But behind the fear was the knowledge of the unpredictable element that marked the man of God, because he was led by the Spirit. It appears that Paul too was accused by some of being fickle because he did not carry through his original plans (2 Cor. 1 : 15–18).

This unpredictable element may serve to re-assure the intercessor. The mysterious union of the Spirit and the believer in the activity of prayer subjects him to a subtle temptation. He begins to wonder whether what he had assumed was the ac-tivity of the Holy Spirit might not after all be merely psychological. What you have learned to expect, by a kind of auto-suggestion is brought to pass. 'Is this the Holy Spirit, or is it just me?' It is here that he is helped by this unpredictable element. He soon finds that these operations are not always according to his own preconceptions but often quite contrary to them. The conviction that this is indeed the Holy Spirit is further strength-ened when, in retrospect, the reasonableness and rightness of the Spirit's leadings are confirmed.

We shall notice this unpredictable element ap-pearing in these further testimonies. The first is from one who had been praying for some time for his own locality, and in particular about a certain property that the Lord had shown him was needed for the work of God.

'The Lord has told me that the time has now come to wage a spiritual war for the possession of——. I was impressed that there was Satanic opposition to its release, and that there was a need for sustained prayer in the Spirit. I had never re-ceived such a prayer commission before and I asked the Lord to show me how I was to fulfil it. Was I to undertake this alone? Was I to set aside a certain time each day? If not, what priority was I to give to this intercession? The Lord's answer was clear and simple. I was to walk this path alone, and He would burden me when He wanted me to give myself to prayer in this way, and then everything else was to be laid aside.

'Next morning I woke at 5 a.m. with slight stomach discomfort. My first thought was that I should have been up at 4.00 for special intercession that I have once a week at that time. I jumped up, thinking, "Better late than never." Not until I was on my knees did I realize that this prayer vigil was not due till the following morning! I knew at once why the Lord had got me up at that early hour, and could not but smile at the way He had done it. A time of praise was followed by fervent intercession in tongues. This in turn gave way to a convulsion of dry rapid sobbing, all inward and almost silent. I was conscious of battling with the powers of darkness. I saw that specific intercession was also needed for the release of the finance—a considerable sum—for the obtaining of the property. I then had a repeat of the intercession, first praise, then tongues, and finally wordless praying, only this time I knew that this was for the necessary finance. This second time the wordless praying was quite different; instead of dry sobbing there was an inner groaning or yearning, a kind of travail to bring forth.

'The pattern has continued much the same from day to day, first for the release of the property and then for the finances involved. Almost every day the Spirit has moved upon me to pray in this way, and sometimes I have had the burden more than once in the day. The constraint to lay aside what I am doing is not usually strong, and I have to be very sensitive to the Spirit. Once or twice I have been gently reproved because I missed hearing His voice—too preoccupied! Occasionally I have got down before the Lord expecting the intercession to come upon me, and nothing has happened, but the Lord has given it later. This assures me it is not of me, and is also a salutary reminder that the Spirit does not work to order.

'Looking back over this first month there has been no noticeable lengthening in the periods of intercession, but a definite intensifying of the Spirit's activity. This has been very gradual and like watching the waves when the tide is coming in, one can only see the advance over a period. Sometimes the wordless praying is marked by a holy violence that shakes my whole body and leaves me for the moment breathless and exhausted. I begin to understand what Jesus meant when He said of His kingdom, "The violent take it by force."

'One day at the end of the first week when the Spirit's moving was becoming more powerful, I was surprised when His sobbing within me was as gentle as the summer rain. I waited for "Part Two" (for the finance) and it didn't come, and what a comfort and confirmation to find I couldn't produce it! Instead I received a gentle anointing, more a kind of "presence" pervading my being, as though the Spirit was saying, "I want to get fuller possession of you." With this, several things from the Scriptures were opened to my mind in a new and wonderful way. Then, without the usual preliminaries of praise and tongues, I went straight into deep silent prayer for the release of the finance.

'I have sensed in the Spirit that the sobbing in the first part of my intercession indicates an initial phase in the Spirit's work, while the groaning of the second part indicates that His work is more advanced. The Spirit has warned me of the necessity of a pure heart and right motives in praying for this money. Now the sobbing usually ends up with groaning and travail, with occasional wailing or deep sighing in the Spirit. The amazing thing is that all this is inward and virtually silent—very necessary in view of my domestic circumstances. I don't think that anyone outside my door would hear anything.

'One morning I found myself in an agony of prayer pressing down on the floor with my hands and virtually lifting myself off my knees. This happened three times, and each time I found myself saying, "I break it in the name of the Lord." Then a sense of relief, of finality, as though something really had been broken, though I do not know what. I am encouraged to believe that a definite milestone has been passed. Whatever is happening in the unseen realm, the Lord is certainly working in the outward situation. We see so many changes, none big in itself, but together adding up to something quite impressive. In addition the Lord is certainly working in me. There is a renewing of faith, a new sensitivity to the Spirit, and a deepening of my whole prayer life. No doubt there is a good way to go yet, but I am waxing strong in faith for the ultimate fulfilment. All this is the Lord's doing, and marvellous in my eyes.'

Finally, there is an account by one who has been for many years engaged in a ministry of intercession. She writes first of the way the Lord prepared her over the years:

'Though I had known intercession before, I had no knowledge of the type of intercession into which God desired to take me. God had to take me like a little child and teach me right from the beginning. First I was taught to know the Holy Spirit in such a deep, deep fellowship, not only to know how to yield to His moving, but much more to know Him personally, with a great love and appreciation.

'Then I was brought into a wonderful relationship with the Father, to know Him with a very deep personal knowledge until I understood something of His great love and compassion, His holiness, His justice and His glory. Since then God has begun to bring me into a much deeper relationship with His Son.

'It was about four and a half years ago, the Father again started to bring me in to a deeper place of intercession, after some very difficult years. Though He took me a long way at that time —I was praying alone—He told me He could only take me so far, as the way was too difficult without prayer support. Now He has given me two partners. J. is a university student, K. is a mother with a young daughter and I am middle-aged. God has bound us like a threefold cord, that we might not be broken, as we pray together for His people in these last days. We would rather do this work of intercession than anything else on earth.

'Let me tell you what God did for us one night recently. We started as we always do by being led of the Spirit of God into deep worship and praise. As we worshipped and sought God we became aware that we were again in the secret, hidden place into which God had brought us. This place we had been brought into after months of consistent praying, two, three or more hours a night, four nights a week. It is a special place of hiding and safety from which we can do battle against the powers of darkness for God's people. It is not an end in itself, but a stopping place along the way for a special purpose. This night a brother was with us. B. is a friend who has a similar ministry and knows how to do battle against the enemy.

'At the beginning we did not understand what God was doing, but as we followed the Spirit of God in deeper we became aware of two things. Firstly, there was deep sorrow of spirit with weeping and crying for some of His people who were suffering and in very great need. Who they were we had not yet been shown. Secondly, and running parallel with the sorrow and travail, was an acute awareness that we were up against very strong powers of darkness in this matter. As we continued in the Spirit, K. was shown in the mid-heavens a throne set, with a being enthroned on it. Before

this throne stood a group of demons, armed and
set in battle array. Then we knew we were up
against a "principality". We continued to seek
God, standing on His word with strong praise and
dependance on the redemption of the Lord Jesus
Christ and the triumph of His cross.

'Gradually God showed us for whom we were
praying. Looking down from the heavenly place
we were in, K. could see a number of little grass
huts hidden in a swamp. With deep sorrow and
weeping she told us what God was showing her,
Christians tortured, sick, suffering, hungry, and
hiding in a swamp. To us this bore the witness of
the Spirit upon it. With outstretched hands we
pleaded their cause before the Father and stayed
pleading until He had filled our hands with supplies
for their need. But we were in heavenly places and
they were in a swamp. We could not take these
supplies ourselves. We sought God until He reminded us of His angel messengers and permitted
us to ask Him to send them in our stead. Then we
could hand over, as it were, to the appointed angels
the succour God had given us for our brethren and
wait until the angel contingent was on its way to
meet their need.

'As we waited God was showing us a further
need requiring urgent attention. K. saw a Christian
who had been tortured, mercilessly beaten and
kicked into insensibility, being dragged along the
ground. His head hung in unconsciousness and he
had a mortal wound in his left side. Much of the
pain of his suffering she felt in her own body so
that she cried out in pain. With this before us we

cried to God for this brother. God showed us that this was His "key man" and He needed him alive, but he was so badly injured that apart from a miracle of God he could not survive. With many tears and groanings that were too deep for words, we sought God for our beloved brother.

'After we had prayed in this way for some time we became aware that J. was speaking, almost in a whisper. Then our weeping hushed; we waited before God while the Holy Spirit took of the heart's cry of one who, in his unconsciousness could not speak for himself, and poured it out to the Father through J. as she lay, not on a filthy prison floor, but on the carpet thousands of miles away. As we listened and marvelled at the beauty of this man's spirit, tears streamed down our faces. We heard, whispered and halting, as from the lips of one whose physical life was ebbing fast, "I'm so tired. I'm . . . so . . . tired. Oh, Father . . . I'm so tired I just want to die. I just want to die. Please take me home, Father. I don't think I can stand any more. Take me home, Father . . . nevertheless . . . not . . . my will . . . but yours be done." Then the soul seemed to struggle for a little while before words came again, "I shall . . . not . . . die. I shall not die but I shall live. I shall not die but I shall live to declare Thy works, O Lord." Then there followed such an outpouring of that dear man's soul in long passages of Scripture that we knew it was not J. who was speaking.

'Suddenly, breaking into the flow of Scripture came a cry of fear—"Oh, God, I'm so cold. What is happening to me? Is this death? Oh, my God, save me! Now I know you want me to live—but this coldness, it's creeping up over me. Oh, God, save me." Realizing what was happening to our brother, the three of us who were watching took this matter up with the Father, urgently, desperately, until the Holy Spirit poured faith into our hearts and gave us the authority to rebuke the angel of death and turn him back. When the Holy Spirit had finished, and the words which poured from J.'s lips were psalms of praise in the midst of suffering, it was given to others of us to join in and lift the heart's cry of our unconscious brother to God, "Father, I believe you. Father, I believe you."

'At last we knew the Holy Spirit had gained from the Father that which He desired and we were freed from our task. We rested in the presence of the Lord and could now speak to each other again. K. said, "One thing I don't understand is the way he was dressed. He was clothed in a golden garment which covered his head and his whole body right down to his feet like a space suit." B. replied, "Yes, Sister, he was clothed in a garment of faith. Remember 1 Peter 1:7, 'The trial of your faith, being much more precious than of gold that perisheth, though it be tried by fire . . .' That's how God saw him, clothed with faith." '

In concluding this chapter it must be stressed that such remarkable experiences as we have just recorded are comparatively rare, even among those who are constantly praying in the Spirit. Nevertheless it should stimulate our faith to know that God can and does work in such ways today. Though it may never be given to us to experience such visions and revelations, it *is* given to us to intercede in the Spirit—to yield ourselves and trust ourselves to His gracious control—to expect that He will pray through us. Then, whether or not we have dramatic experiences, we shall know with deep joy and thanksgiving that we have prayed in the Spirit, and God who sees in secret will reward us openly.

## 18

# TILL BREAK OF DAY

LIKE the theme of some musical composition the wonderful truth that 'the Spirit helps us in our weakness' in prayer has recurred again and again throughout this book. Nowhere else in the Bible are we given such an insight into the way the Holy Spirit works in the heart of the believer who prays in the Spirit as we have in Romans 8: 26, 27. We must now set the whole matter in perspective by pointing out that Spirit-inspired praying is not really the theme of Romans 8, and what Paul tells us about it is only incidental to his grand objective. To this great apostle praying in the Spirit is not the end—and we must not make it that—it is simply the means to the end. What then is the end?

The theme of Romans is 'the gospel of God' (1 : 1). But what length and breadth, depth and height we find here as the epistle unfolds. It could hardly be summarized by 'Come to Jesus and be forgiven'! After a thorough unfolding of man's condemnation, Paul moves on to the ground of his justification, his sanctification, and his glorification. It is in this very Chapter 8 that the emphasis changes from the believer's present sanctification to his future glorification. The transition in the apostle's development of his theme is not sudden but gradual, as one colour in the rainbow merges into the next. The goal, then, is the glory of the age to come.

Let us now read carefully verses 1–25 of Romans 8 and try to grasp the trend of Paul's argument. Having spoken of life in the Spirit, he declares (verse 11) that the Spirit who now dwells in us will (future tense) give life to our mortal bodies. Though there is a present application of this in a physical strengthening and quickening, the apostle has future resurrection primarily in view. This truth, that the present blessing of the Spirit is both a preparation for and a guarantee of the resurrection or redemption of our bodies and the title to our future inheritance, occurs in several epistles:

> We ourselves, who have the first fruits of the Spirit, groan inwardly as we wait for adoption as sons, the redemption of our bodies (Rom. 8:23).
> Here indeed we groan, and long to put on our heavenly dwelling (resurrection body) ... He who has prepared us for this very thing is God, who has given us the Spirit as a guarantee (2 Cor. 5:2, 5).
> You ... were sealed with the promised Holy Spirit, which is the guarantee of our inheritance until we acquire possession of it (Eph. 1:13, 14). And do not grieve the Holy Spirit of God, in whom you were sealed for the day of redemption (Eph. 4:30).

What Paul is saying in verse 11 of Romans 8, is that the Holy Spirit within us—the very same

Spirit that raised Jesus from the dead—will also raise us up. Just as the lunar module speeding towards its historic first landing on the moon had residing within it the power to bring it back from the moon at the touch of a button, so we have within us, in the person of the life-giving Spirit, the power that will one day effect our resurrection.

The Holy Spirit, continues Paul (verses 15–17), has delivered us from a slavish spirit of fear and given us instead a spirit of sonship. He inspires within us the cry, 'Abba! Father!' He brings to us the consciousness of being God's children, and that implies heirship—'heirs of God and fellow-heirs with Christ'. As a young heir to some important title is specially trained for his future responsibilities, so the Holy Spirit is teaching and training us for the day when we shall enter upon our inheritance.

Now the apostle warms to his subject. In thrilling terms he describes (verses 18–23) what this inheritance will mean for us and for the whole universe. Suffering he has certainly known in full measure (and for him there was more to come), but in his opinion it is 'not worth comparing with the glory that is to be revealed to us' (verse 18). Notice how he relates the sufferings to 'this present time' (cp. Acts 14:22; 2 Cor. 4:17), and the glory (in its full manifestation, of course) 'to be revealed to us' in the coming age. This is the trail blazed by the Pioneer of our salvation. He trod the pathway of suffering, that through death and resurrection He might enter into His glory. (Luke 24:46; 1 Pet. 1:11).

What then is the glory? It is the revealing of the sons of God. Paul paints the picture of the creation groaning with desire, breathless with expectation, for this moment for which all the past ages were but a preparation, when God will display to the wondering eyes of the whole universe His master-piece. Poets and hymnists have used their art to try to describe the glory of that scene when Christ returns, but so often they have missed the point Paul is emphasizing here. He is not to be revealed *without us*. When that day dawns and that hour strikes—and only God knows when that will be—when the heir of the universe steps on to the dais, He will not be alone, His fellow heirs will be with Him. Certainly He is coming to be glorified, but it is, 'in His saints ... in all who have believed' (2 Thes. 1:10). The world will indeed see a glorified Man, but that Man will comprise not only Christ the Head but also the church, His body; not only the Bridegroom but also the Bride, invested with the beauty, dignity and glory of her Lord. As Paul puts it in verse 17, if we 'suffer with Him' now, we shall 'be glorified with Him' then.

As man's sin brought futility and bondage to the whole creation, so man's final redemption will effect its release. This will be when the sons of God are revealed. It is for this that the creation waits with eager longing (verses 19–21). It is for this that it groans as a woman in travail (verse 22). This then is the goal towards which we press. This is the glorious hope in which we were saved; a hope that is not yet seen, not yet realized, but for which we patiently wait.

This waiting, however, is not for us a waiting of inactivity, for we are sharing the travail of the rest of creation for the birth of the new age. 'We ourselves, who have the first fruits of the Spirit, groan inwardly as we wait for adoption as sons, the redemption of our bodies' (verse 23). As we wait we groan. This groaning, as has already been pointed out, is intimately connected with the first fruits of the Spirit, and so to be distinguished from the groaning of the rest of creation. It is a groaning of the Spirit in us. Thus praying in the Spirit, especially this inarticulate praying, has an indispensable part to play in the birth of the new age.

We commonly think of this present age as 'the age of the Spirit', or 'the age of service', and the coming age as 'the age of rest'. This may be misleading. The expressions which the New Testament uses in relation to the blessing of the Spirit are deeply suggestive, for they imply that a much richer age of the Spirit is yet to come. Here in verse 23 we are said to have 'the first fruits of the Spirit'. Now first fruits are but the foretaste of the harvest that is to follow. How disappointed the Israelite would be if having gathered the first fruits there was no main crop to follow. His barns would be well nigh empty. Have we realized that the power of the Spirit displayed at Pentecost, and demonstrated in the ministries of Peter, Paul, Stephen and others, is after all, only first fruits? What then will the harvest be like when the new age is born?

Elsewhere Paul speaks of the same blessing of the Spirit as 'the guarantee' (R.S.V.) or 'earnest of the Spirit' (A.V. and R.V.) (see 2 Cor. 1:22, 5:5;

Eph. 1:13, 14). The basic meaning of the word is
'earnest money', just like the 10% downpayment
or deposit that is nowadays paid when a house is
purchased. It is the guarantee of the full sum. What
vendor would be satisfied if the 10% deposit was
all he received? If the pentecostal outpouring was
but a downpayment, what will the full payment
be like?

Those who have received the baptism in the
Holy Spirit and the wonderful gifts that accom-
pany or follow it, are said to have merely 'tasted
the heavenly gift . . . and the powers of the age to
come' (Heb. 6:4, 5). If what we now have is but a
foretaste, glorious as it is, of that which in its fullness is reserved for the coming age, what will the
banquet be like? No wonder the great apostle
thrilled at the prospect of 'the glory that is to be
revealed to us'. We shall certainly need redeemed
bodies, resurrected and transformed, to be fit
vessels for such an inflow of divine power and
glory. One wonders how believers who now recoil
in fear from any supernatural manifestations of
the Spirit will fare in that coming day? If the
downpayment is too much for them, how will they
handle the full payment? If they are put off by the
taste, how will they stomach the feast?

All this accords with the other teaching in the
New Testament, that this age is only a probation-
ary period for the believer, in preparation for the
true age of service to come (Mat. 25:14–30; Luke
19:11–27). In the parable of the pounds the master
on his return told the first servant, whose one
pound had gained ten pounds, 'You have been

faithful in a very little, you shall have authority over ten cities' (Luke 19:17). Had he said to his servant, 'Have authority over ten *houses*' that would have implied a greatly increased responsibility, but he said 'ten cities'. From stewarding a modest sum of a few pounds which his master describes as 'a very little', he finds himself ruler of a sizeable province of his master's kingdom. The principle on which the Lord will determine His appointments in that day is now operating. 'He who is faithful in a very little is faithful also in much.' The day of reckoning must soon come. Let us look to the talent and to the pound entrusted to us.

Is not the ministry of intercession an important part of our stewardship? As we pray in the Spirit are we not trading in the spiritual realm and producing eternal profits? Our Lord Jesus has become the first fruits of those that sleep. He is the guarantee that we shall one day have glorified bodies like His. Has His glorification terminated His intercession? No, indeed, one would think that it had enlarged it. For now, as our great High Priest 'He always lives to make intercession' for us (Heb. 7:25). May not our glorification also open up far greater possibilities in the ministry of intercession when the kingdom of our God and His Christ has fully come? If we are unfaithful in the 'very little' now, how can He entrust us with 'much' then?

It is essential that we rid our minds of any idea that intercession is a special ministry to which God calls a favoured few. It was not to any select class, but to disciples in general, that Jesus told the parable 'to the effect that they ought always to pray and not lose heart' (Luke 18 : 1–8). Whatever else our ministry may involve the Lord would remind us that we 'ought always to pray'. Similarly the apostle Paul was not addressing a particular class in the church at Thessalonica, but believers in general, when he said, 'Pray constantly' (1 Thes. 5 : 17). And those thus addressed were not seasoned warriors of many years standing, but new converts who were little more than babes in Christ. Whether young or old in the faith, intercession is not an optional extra.

The message of this book, however, is that we are not only commanded to pray, not only commanded to pray without ceasing but also to 'pray in the Holy Spirit'. The apostle Jude sandwiches this between two other commands—'build yourselves up on your most holy faith' and 'keep yourselves in the love of God' (verses 20, 21). The importance of these two we all recognize, but the middle one is seldom understood and therefore neglected. Paul goes even farther than Jude, for he says that we are to pray in the Spirit 'always' (A.V.) or 'at all seasons' (R.V., R.S.V.). This disposes for ever of the idea that this is a special kind of praying reserved for the favoured few, or one that we exercise on special occasions. It is of course the only standard of praying the New Testament recognizes. Anything less is subnormal.

Is there within you a real desire to be led into a ministry of praying in the Spirit, even to know that groaning in travail of which the apostle speaks? In that case we cannot leave Romans 8 without mentioning the three keys that Paul gives us in this chapter which are essential to the opening up of this ministry.

In verses 12 and 13 he speaks of the mortification of the body:

> So then, brethren, we are debtors, not to the flesh, to live according to the flesh—for if you live according to the flesh you will die, but if by the Spirit you put to death the deeds of the body you will live.

Prayer in the Spirit spells death to the flesh. Being almost entirely a secret ministry there is nothing here in which the flesh can glory. How true it is that the desires of the flesh are against the Spirit, and the desires of the Spirit are against the flesh '. . . to prevent you from doing what you would' (Gal. 5:17). This is the primary reason why many never enter this realm. The flesh strongly objects and they weakly give in. But Paul says, 'You don't owe the flesh anything! Don't give in to it, put it to death, mortify the deeds of the body!' That is key number one.

In verses 17 and 18 he speaks about *suffering*:

> And if children, then heirs, heirs of God and fellow heirs with Christ, provided we suffer with Him in order that we may also be glorified with Him. I consider that the sufferings of this present time are not worth comparing with the glory that is to be revealed to us.

Travail and bringing forth inevitably involve a measure of suffering. People may talk nowadays about painless childbirth, but there is no such thing in the spiritual realm. I am not suggesting that we are called to suffer as Paul did. It is a question of recognizing that we are called to suffer (Phil. 1 : 29; 1 Thes. 3 : 3) and so of arming ourselves with such a mind (1 Pet. 4 : 1). If we do not cultivate the mind to suffer we shall never be a vehicle through whom the Spirit can travail. Naturally we recoil from this, but that merely emphasizes the need of the third key.

In verses 24 and 25 he speaks of our *future hope* :

> For in this hope we were saved. Now hope that is seen is not hope. For who hopes for what he sees? But if we hope for what we do not see, we wait for it with patience.

It was the vision of the coming glory that sustained our Saviour in His night of travail, 'who for the joy that was set before Him endured the cross, despising the shame'. Similarly Paul tells us that he did not consider that his sufferings were worth comparing with the glory that was to come. This is our hope, and 'in this hope we were saved'. Let the Holy Spirit once set that hope on fire in our souls, and we too will ever after call our sufferings 'our light affliction', and declare that it is not worth comparing with the glory. This hope has yet to fire the hearts of God's people. When it does it will become the major incentive in the final proclamation of the gospel of the kingdom to all the nations of the earth, as well as in the producing of that prayer travail which will give birth to the coming age.

As the darkness deepens and the dawn of Christ's appearing draws steadily nearer, let us give ourselves to this vital ministry. If our priorities need adjusting let us adjust them. If some good and desirable things have to go, let them go. Has not the good ever been the enemy of the best? 'The night is far gone, the day is at hand. Let us then cast off the works of darkness and put on the armour of light.' Let us believe that the great interceding Spirit will pray through us, until the day dawn. The world has yet to see such a manifestation of the glory of God that can only come through a church, cleansed and purified, praying in the power of the Holy Spirit.

This book was produced by the Christian Literature Crusade. We hope it has been helpful to you in living the Christian life. CLC is a literature mission with ministry in over 40 countries worldwide. If you would like to know more about us, or are interested in opportunities to serve with a faith mission, we invite you to write to:

Christian Literature Crusade
P.O. Box 1449
Fort Washington, PA 19034